Victorian Jewelry

Victorian Jewelry

UNEXPLORED TREASURES

GINNY REDINGTON DAWES

CORINNE DAVIDOV

PHOTOGRAPHS BY TOM DAWES

ABBEVILLE PRESS PUBLISHERS

NEW YORK LONDON

Editor: Jacqueline Decter
Art Director: Renée Khatami
Designer: Deborah Glasserman
Copy Chief: Robin James
Production Supervisor: Hope Koturo

First paperback edition
10 9 8 7 6 5 4 3 2 1
ISBN 0-7892-0868-7

A previous edition of this book was cataloged as follows:

Library of Congress Cataloging-in-Publication Data
Dawes, Ginny Redington.
    Victorian jewelry: unexplored treasures/ Ginny Redington Dawes,
    Corinne Davidov:
    photographs by Tom Dawes.
    p. cm
Includes bibliographical reference
    and index.
1. Jewelry, Victorian. I. Cavidov, Corinne.
    II. Title.
NK7309.85V53.D38 1991
739.27'09'034—dc20   90-48329
                                    CIP

For bulk and premium sales and for text adoption procedures, write to Customer Service Manager, Abbeville Press, 137 Varick Street, New York, NY 10013 or call 1-800-Artbook.

Contents

Acknowledgments

Our heartfelt gratitude to our husbands, Tom Dawes and Ted Davidov, for their unstinting interest, encouragement, and assistance, and to our special friends, Lesley Miller, Julie Seitzman, Pam and Doug Brown, and Joan Maxwell, who shared their knowledge and opened their collections to us. The realization of this book could not have been accomplished without the kindness and expertise of the many collectors and dealers who graciously loaned us their finest treasures: Brian and Lynn Holmes, Nicky Butler, Simon Wilson, Olivia Gerrish, Joanna Elton, Linda Morgan, Madeleine Popper, Jacqueline Jacoby, Noel Gibson, Allison Massey, Olivia Collings, Ted Donohoe, Lindy Conyngham-Hynes, and Paul Lesbirel, all from London; and Joan Munves, Julie Seymour, Marcie Imberman, Ellen Israel, Edith Weber, Barry Weber, Angela Kramer, Renee Lewis, Fran Cohen, Amy Brown, Patricia Funt, Terry Rodgers, Korby Britton, Justine Mehlman, Jackie Smelkinson, Marcia Moylan, Benita Berman, Caroline Finberg, Barbara Jackson, Betty Brooks, Robin Mullin, Patty Goetz, Lala Schnee, Antonia and Gary Blucher, Wendy Jachman, and Eleanor Davidov, all from this side of the Atlantic. Grateful thanks to those who helped us with our research: Tin Shue Chin of the Library of Congress, Neil Clark of the Hunterian Museum of Glasgow, Kate Urquhart, Karen Myerberg, and Kathryn Koring; to our experts in their fields: Luciano Delvillar (our wonder-working jeweler), Michael Ward (a most knowledgeable lapidary), and Fred Schwartz (our lawyer); to the foremost champion of our project, Abbeville's Walton Rawls; to our editor, Jackie Decter, our designer Deborah Glasserman, art director Renée Khatami, and Jane Lahr for their continuing enthusiasm. Last but not least, a bow to the woman who made this book possible—Queen Victoria!

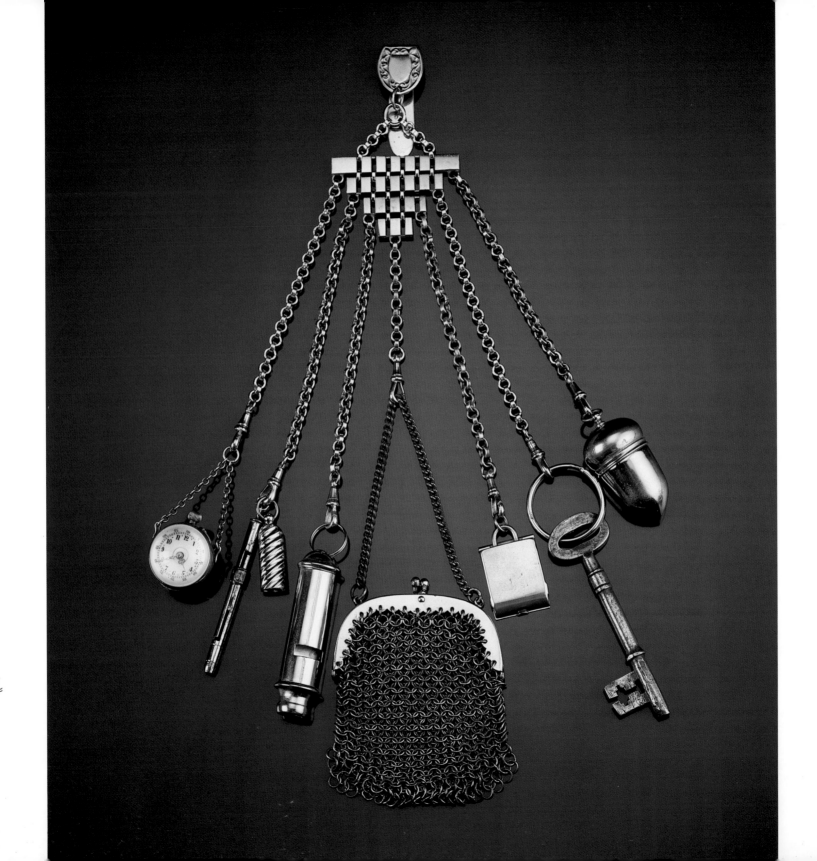

Introduction

Until recently, Victorian jewelry was not our cup of tea. It conjured up images of tightly corseted matrons bedecked in fussy froufrou, archaic hair combs, and an endless proliferation of cameos, and seemed to have little relevance to the twentieth century. But along London's Portobello Road one Saturday morning we discovered that there was more to Victorian jewelry than the delicately elaborate adornments of gold and precious stones that are inevitably associated with the Victorian era (1837–1901). What we discovered was the world of Victorian "secondary" jewelry—bold, playful, and romantic; modern, oversized, and fashionably faddish. It was jewelry that was worn mostly by day and that was less expensive because it was made from nonprecious materials such as stone, coal, hair, steel, papier-mâché, and aluminum. It was jewelry that took chances, running the gamut from the daring to the whimsical, and it was accessible: worn by the middle classes then and, hallelujah, affordable to the middle classes now!

This jewelry did away with our preconceived notions of the Victorian era. Through it, we were able to envision a time and a culture as it was then, the workings of a civilization different from ours but in many ways very much the same. How did Victorians feel about love and life? Much as we do—they, too, were sentimental fools! They, too, had materialistic tendencies! Like us, they were inventive in the face of the pressing problems of the day: the use of the "vinaigrette," for example, a wearable little container made to hold an aromatic preparation from which nineteenth-century women could inhale as they walked the garbage-strewn cobblestones of industrial cities. Like us, they had an abiding fascination with gadgetry, as evidenced by the "chatelaine," the Victorian equivalent of the Swiss army knife. Their fads, too, could be

Chromium chatelaine, c. 1895 (facing page).

Aluminum and gilt metal bracelet, c. 1850.

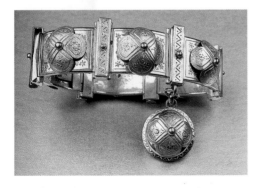

George IV silver vinaigrettes, c. 1820.

Mid-Victorian Scottish agate belt bracelets, c. 1855 (facing page).

Georgian painted eye miniatures (below).

rather outlandish, as some of the more bizarre, talismanic aspects of pre-Victorian and Victorian jewelry demonstrate: from attractive/ repulsive "hair jewelry" (mourning jewelry woven of a loved one's hair) to the beautiful but chilling "eye jewelry" (exquisitely painted miniatures of a loved one's eyes).

Because most budding collectors have neither the resources nor the connections for finding museum-quality Victorian jewelry, we decided to concentrate on jewelry that can still be found and purchased today. So, from some of the most eclectic dealers and collectors in both America and Great Britain, we have chosen the finest available examples of these nonprecious "gems" of Victorian jewelry with particular accent on the unexplored treasures of the period, such as cut steel and tortoiseshell piqué, which are much prized today for their beauty and workmanship and because they have become "endangered species." We have delighted in the timeless, elegant simplicity of Victorian silver jewelry and have marveled at the glorious color and style of "Scottish" agate, the amazing modernity of niello (dark gray enamel-like inlay on silver), and the stark black beauty of the fossilized wood known as Whitby jet.

Believing firmly in the symbiosis of today's fashions and yesterday's finery, we have placed special emphasis on pieces that are wearable today: those with a modern touch or a beauty too timeless to be relegated to a dusty drawer.

Fortuitously, since we began working on this project, there has been a tremendous resurgence of interest in the Victorian period. Collectors and laymen alike are flocking in increasing numbers to booths featuring Victorian jewelry at antique shows. Ralph Lauren is promoting Victorian agate and silver to be worn in fresh new ways with his

Victorian tartan-wear bracelet and brooch, made out of papier-mâché.

tweeds and jodhpurs. Fine department stores are dedicating extensive counter space to Victorian secondary jewelry. Magazines such as *Victoria*, articles in *Newsweek* and *Time*, and spreads in *Vogue* and *HG* report the return to favor of everything Victorian, from fashion to furnishings to morals! Yet there are few books that do more than touch on the categories of Victorian jewelry that we explore in depth here. Because of all this, we hope *Victorian Jewelry: Unexplored Treasures* will be worth its weight in gold.

The young Queen Victoria, a portrait by Herbert L. Smith.

he Victorian period began in 1837 with the coronation of England's Queen Victoria. Only eighteen years old at the time, she already had a tremendous presence. Her charisma was to grow with every year of her reign, which ended with her death in 1901.

Victoria was undoubtedly the greatest influence of her time, and what she loved, her country loved. What Victoria loved was Albert, sentiment, and jewelry, in that order!

With her betrothal, the whole of England fell in love, and the atmosphere in the early Victorian period (1837–1860) was as romantic as it was ever to be. Styles in dress and jewelry reflected this romanticism: diaphanous lightweight gowns, delicate gold and gemstone parures (matched sets), strands of seed pearls, and small lockets. Because

Delicate early Victorian carnelian and pearl
earrings set in gold.

Mid-nineteenth-century silver "faith, hope, and charity" charm.

of Victoria's love of nature, and of the Scottish landscape in particular, naturalistic themes abounded, with delicate floral-spray brooches, hair combs of tortoiseshell in the shape of branches, and bracelets made of silver and stones from Scottish mountain streams. Victoria was a religious monarch, and many pieces of jewelry made during her reign had religious significance: crosses for faith, anchors for hope, hearts for charity, and serpents for eternity. Sentimental symbolism was at its peak, and jewelry made from a loved one's hair became more popular than ever.

The early Victorian period produced a passion for the Middle Ages. There were medieval costume balls and jousting tournaments, in France as well as in England, in which the participants actually wore antique armor. Jewelry of the period reflected this enthusiasm for medievalism, and Gothic Revival finery proliferated.

The early Victorian period also coincided with the height of the Industrial Revolution, and more goods were being made accessible to more people than ever before. The Great Exhibition at the Crystal Palace in London opened in 1851 and, for the first time in history, the world viewed a multinational display of expertly crafted goods. (It must be pointed out that although many people associate Victorian jewelry with England, much of it was produced on the Continent, particularly in France.) Jewelry made from unusual nonprecious metals, such as cut steel and aluminum, came to the fore and convinced European nobility that all that glittered was not, and did not need to be, gold.

The mid-, or high, Victorian period (1860–1885) had a distinctly different flavor from the sentimental romantic period. Victoria's down-to-earth, solid, sensible values inspired a similar way of thinking. Dresses became larger and more dignified (the crinoline, or hooped petticoat, was in vogue during the 1860s), and jewelry followed suit. The design influences were architectural and archaeological. Neoclassical motifs such as shells and rosettes were used with increasing frequency. Necklaces and earrings sported fringe and Etruscan beading or granulation. Very few new designs were created, makers seemingly content to borrow from the Greek and Etruscan classics, influenced by Italian master goldsmiths such as Castellani and Giuliano.

This was also the heartbreaking period of Prince Albert's untimely death and Victoria's inconsolable mourning. The nation grieved along with her, and mourning clothes and jewelry came into style. Only jet was worn at court following Albert's death, which stimulated the Whitby jet market and engendered the manufacture of the many jet substitutes: bog oak, gutta-percha, "French jet," and tortoiseshell.

In the 1870s, the new Aesthetic Movement gained favor. Inspired by the art and philosophy of the Pre-Raphaelites, it promoted jewelry and fashions that had a sparse new simplicity. Naturalistic designs abounded, but now with a decidedly Oriental flavor. The popularity of japonaiserie, as it was called, was considerable, and thousands of

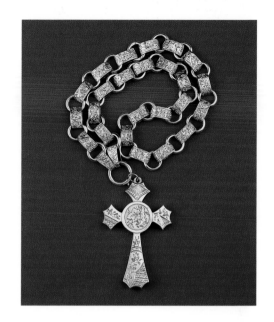

Silver chain and cross with gold overlay in the japonaiserie style, c. 1870 (above).

A late Victorian jet souvenir brooch from Whitby Abbey (left).

A selection of jewelry from Frankfurt, Germany, as illustrated in a catalog of the Great Exhibition of 1851 (facing page).

PRUSSIA, No. 411, p. 1073.
ORNAMENTAL JEWELLERY. J. F. BACKES & CO., *Hanau.*

Pl. 257.

brooches, lockets, and bracelets with asymmetrical designs flooded the market.

The mid-Victorian period ended with a relaxation of the mourning code and the rise of the silver jewelry industry. Heavy lockets and chains and wide, hinged bangle bracelets were favored for daytime wear, as was the silver love brooch, an inexpensive mass-produced item that appealed to the working classes. The end of this period saw the beginnings of sport or novelty jewelry that women wore with their riding habits or golf costumes.

The late Victorian period (1885–1901) saw women moving out of the home and into the world. Traditional notions were rejected and young women embraced the modern age wholeheartedly. They became more active, more aggressive, and more socially and politically aware. They repudiated high Victorian taste, and, as a result, fashions changed dramatically to lighter, simpler, more tailored garments. And as for accessories: no more hearts and flowers. Simple, minimal jewelry in materials such as niello and gunmetal were the order of the day, precursors of the new Edwardian era just around the corner.

Stack of niello hinged bangle bracelets; the bottom one is dated 1883.

Silver

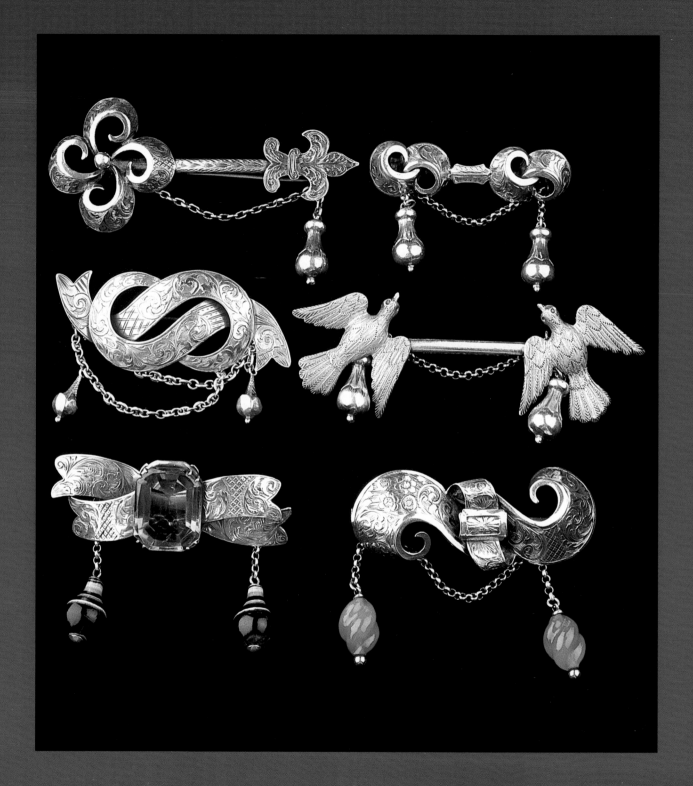

oday there is hardly a collector of antique jewelry who does not desire to own a piece of Victorian silver jewelry, but this was not always so. Even in its own time, Victorian silver jewelry was disdained by the upper classes, though worn frequently by those lower on the economic scale, unmarried women, and children. That even those without means or standing wore jewelry at all was due largely to Queen Victoria's penchant for adornment. Throughout the entire Victorian period, one can trace the Queen's influence on taste and fashion, an influence that encompassed all classes.

As abundant as Victorian silver jewelry is today, it is hard to realize that silver once was a material rebuffed for its tarnishability. The speed with which silver tarnished was, in fact, a new development in

Silver safety brooches by Ellis of Exeter and Hilliard & Thomason, c. 1850.

nineteenth-century London, a result of air pollution caused by the Industrial Revolution. Sulfur dioxide in the air oxidized silver, which lost favor because it was simply too hard to clean.

Although the majority of Victorian silver jewelry was made in the last two decades of the Victorian period, especially from 1888 to 1901, the early and mid-Victorian periods brought forth some beautifully engraved silver jewelry manufactured in Devonshire and Birmingham, and these signed and hallmarked pieces, some of them extremely rare, are prized by collectors today.

Notable among companies that produced silver jewelry at this time was Ellis and Sons of Exeter, whose jewelry attracted tremendous attention at the Great Exhibition of 1851. Henry Samuel Ellis was the inventor of the "safety brooch," which was expertly designed with a completely secure catch. Patented in 1847, it utilized a clever safety bolt that slid back and forth by way of a spring, to secure the pin back. Some of Ellis's brooches were made of two separate but complementary

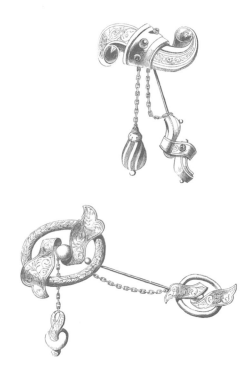

Ellis safety brooches, as illustrated in a catalog of the Great Exhibition of 1851 (above).

Front and back views of Ellis safety brooches (left).

Fine figural silver brooches of the mid-nineteenth century (above).

Extremely large signed silver acorn brooch by George Unite (GU) (right).

parts joined together by the pin and safety catch on the underside and a decorative chain on the front of the piece that provided extra security. The silver was locally mined at Combmartin in north Devon, and some of Ellis's patrons included Queen Victoria, the queen of the Belgians, and the duke of Devonshire. Hundreds of these brooches were registered by Ellis and Sons and then licensed to Hilliard and Thomason (H&T) and manufactured in Birmingham. The designs were inspired by such contemporary motifs of the day as the strap and buckle, the bowknot, the fleur-de-lis, and doves in flight. Ellis and Sons' most popular design was the "outstretched hand." Pebbles from the local beaches of Devonshire were often used as pendants or inlays to embellish these silver brooches. Unfortunately, the Ellis patent did not prevent competitors from copying the company's designs.

Another well-known silversmith was George Unite of Birmingham, who specialized in flatware as well as jewelry and whose productive career spanned three-quarters of a century. His silver brooches are remarkable for their delicacy and naturalism. One of his most successful designs was the leaf and acorn motif.

Silver and blue-enamel luckenbooth.

Scottish plaid brooches set with citrines and amethysts, used to secure the Scotsman's tartan. All but the brooch in the upper left are eighteenth century (facing page).

Common to the mid-Victorian period were figural silver brooches, often in the shape of anchors, arrows, and hearts, and heavy hinged silver bracelets, many having belt-buckle closures. Some of these hinged bracelets were decorated with gold overlay to stunning effect. On most of these pieces were beautifully executed hand-engravings in floral, leaf, and feather patterns. Although this style of jewelry continued to be fashionable right up to the end of the century, earlier pieces can be distinguished from later versions by the fineness of the engraving and the heaviness of the silver. Less common to the mid-Victorian period were silver earrings of any size or workmanship. Silver necklaces followed the prevailing gold fashions of the day. The most effective are the graceful fringed collars in the Greco-Etruscan style made popular by master goldsmiths such as Castellani and Giuliano.

Silver jewelry of this period was influenced not only by the Classical Revival but also by the Gothic Revival, a movement that reinterpreted medieval designs and symbols, such as the Maltese cross (which was the emblem of the eleventh-century Knights Hospitallers who aided pilgrims in Jerusalem) and the luckenbooth (a brooch of Scottish origin consisting of a heart, or sometimes two hearts entwined, surmounted by a crown, which enjoyed renewed popularity in the eighteenth and nineteenth centuries). These love tokens were called luckenbooths because they were sold as souvenirs from "locked booths" on the High Street in Edinburgh. Inspired by the rediscovery of Celtic/Scottish brooches such as the sixteenth century's Loch Buy Brooch, the nineteenth century saw the rise in popularity of silver jewelry set with a central crystal—either a citrine, amethyst, or "cairngorm," the smoky orange-brown quartz from the Cairngorm mountain range in Scotland. Besides the traditional oversized round silver brooches that held a Scotsman's shoulder plaid in place, jewelers made beautifully engraved citrine-set bracelets, earrings, cape pins, brooches, and, extremely rarely, belts.

The discovery in 1860 of the Comstock Lode in Nevada assured the world of an ample supply of silver at more attractive prices, which, of course, benefited the jewelry industry even though two decades passed before this was truly felt. The increased availability of silver coincided with a new age in fashion brought about by the popularity of the Aesthetic Movement, which espoused simplicity of design and a sparse asymmetrical naturalism. The world was newly enamored of Japanese customs and culture as a result of the trade agreement between the United States and Japan brought about by Commodore Perry in 1854. The followers of the Aesthetic Movement embraced all things Japanese and were especially drawn to the artwork, rich in its imagery and graphic in its love of nature. This mania for japonaiserie reached its peak simultaneously with the renewed popularity of silver jewelry, and the late 1870s saw a most fitting marriage of the two.

During the Aesthetic Movement period, the most significant silver jewelry was heavy silver collars and lockets, which were oval-shaped (or sometimes rectangular) and suspended from chains with large silver

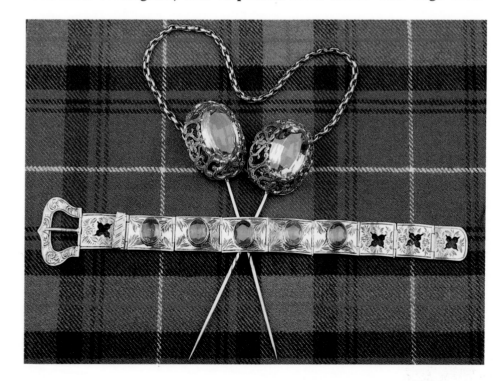

Silver buckle bracelet and cape pins set with citrines.

Rare mid-Victorian engraved silver belt set with cairngorms (right).

Aesthetic Movement silver jewelry decorated with bird motifs, c. 1880 (below).

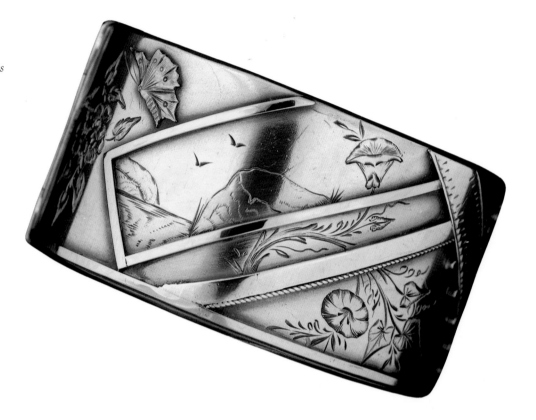

Detail of silver bangle in the japonaiserie style, c. 1870.

Brooch and earrings inspired by the Japanese arts of shakudo and shibuichi, c. 1875 (facing page).

links. Queen Victoria presented a wide silver collar to famed singer Jenny Lind, and in 1878 these chains and lockets became the most fashionable ornaments for everyday wear. Lockets were oversized to accommodate photographs, which were, at that time, still difficult to reduce. The designs on the flattened links and the locket itself were engraved with a delicate simplicity new to the era in endless variations on such Aesthetic Movement themes as fans, cherry blossoms, a single bird or butterfly, bamboo, bulrushes, and storks. There was usually a geometric feeling to the designs, and the focal point was often off center and on the diagonal. Influenced by the Japanese arts of *shakudo* (using alloys of gold and copper) and *shibuichi* (silver and copper), jewelers used overlays and inlays of different-colored golds (yellow and pink) on silver, giving the designs both an Eastern flavor and a three-

A watercolor by Blanche Lindsay of Princess Louise wearing a Giuliano necklace like the one Queen Victoria gave to Jenny Lind.

dimensionality. Some of these lockets were sold in parures (complete sets) displayed in leather cases with matching bangle bracelets, brooches, and earrings. It is interesting to note that while most of the motifs of this period were Oriental, the shape of the jewelry remained distinctly English Victorian.

Heavy silver locket, chain, and earrings in the architectural style of the early 1860s.

The bangle bracelet was the perfect complement for the silver chain and locket, because while appearing heavy and important-looking, it was often hollow and very lightweight. The clean expanse of silver was the perfect medium for gold overlay and decorations in the japonaiserie style.

The nineteenth century witnessed the increasing popularity of the heart padlock—a closure in the shape of a heart, usually with a keyhole and a miniature key that would open the catch. It was used to secure "curb" bracelets, heavy cable-link bracelets made of silver or gold. These were obvious love tokens from suitors who wished to possess the key to their beloved's heart and were used as betrothal jewelry. Both padlocks and chains were often ornately engraved.

By the mid-1880s the fashion was not to wear any daytime jewelry, and the market for silver declined. To stimulate the market, representatives of the jewelry industry in Birmingham wrote to the Princess of Wales exhorting her to wear plain silver daytime jewelry. There was no reply to this entreaty, but, two years later, the jewelry trade was given a great boost when Queen Victoria herself decided to suspend her protracted mourning and wear some silver jewelry to mark the fiftieth anniversary of her reign in 1887. Her ladies-in-waiting and eventually her loyal subjects all followed suit. In 1890 a tax on gold and silver goods was removed, and silver became even more accessible to the masses. Thus began the greatest age yet for the makers of silver novelty jewelry.

Nothing was more popular in the late 1800s than the silver love brooch. Although mass-produced and affordable for even the very poor, it was nevertheless of good quality. Its parts were cut to shape by presses and then soldered together. Decoration was most often impressed by a stamp, although some pieces were hand-engraved or -finished. Many brooches were made with the two-tone or three-tone silver and gold combinations that had become popular during the Aesthetic Movement period.

Silver locket with a central anchor design of gold overlay, c. 1870.

Stack of nineteenth-century silver bangles with gold overlay (facing page).

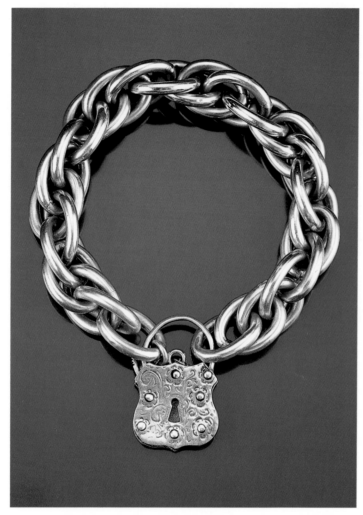

Late Victorian silver padlock bracelets: the one
above is English; the one on the right, American.

Typical silver sentimental pins of the late 1800s.

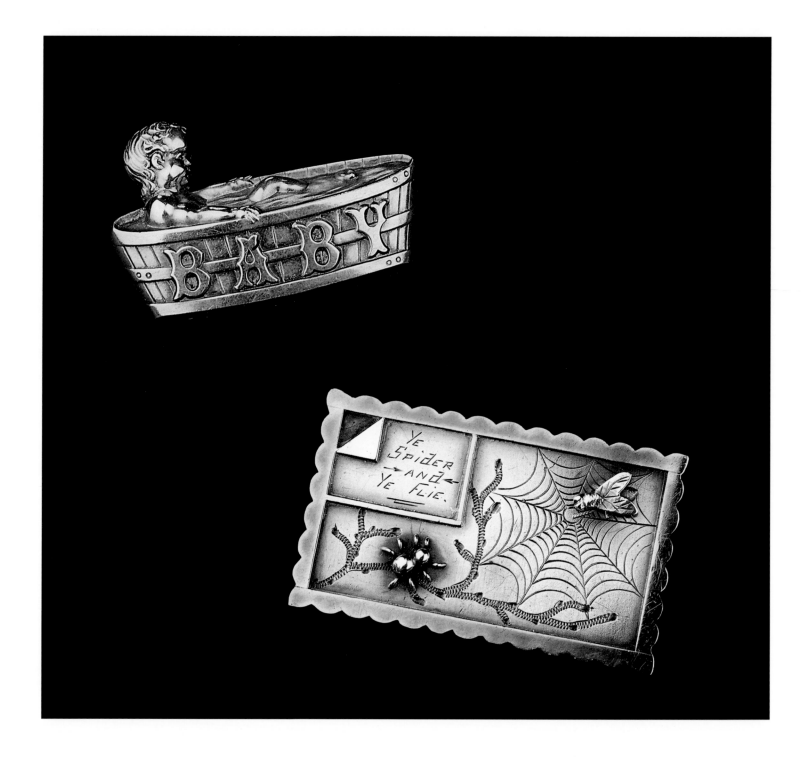

The repertory of love brooch designs was enormous, many of them showing great individuality. Manufacturers of these brooches employed symbolism with great enthusiasm and by 1869 there were three popular dictionaries devoted to interpreting the "language of flowers." A love brooch was often covered with a symbolic message that could be deciphered if one knew the key. For example, ivy leaves stood for friendship, ferns for fascination, bluebells for constancy, and forget-me-nots for remembrance. Besides flowers, there were all manner of amorous and/or religious symbols: lovebirds, cupids, arrows, hearts, hands, ribbons, bows, lovers' knots, and crosses, anchors, and hearts for faith, hope, and charity. Often they bore quaint mottoes like "Ever thine," "Fidelity," or "Gratitude." They were sometimes personalized with names or initials or "Baby." Love brooches often featured the word *Mizpah*, which was taken from a quotation in Genesis that bid the Lord to "watch over me and thee when we are parted one from the other."

In the mid-1880s, women became more liberated and began to indulge in sports, which spawned a whole new category of silver sporting jewelry. In the 1860s the horseshoe brooch had first appeared but it was not immediately popular, as one critic attested in an 1870s issue of the *Art Journal*: "A more outrageous instance in misapplied ingenuity and skill it is impossible to conceive and that any woman would condescend to wear such abominations is more inconceivable still." Nevertheless, by the mid-1870s, this design had captured the fancy of the public, and by the 1880s many an equestrienne was wearing a silver horseshoe on the lapel of her riding habit. By the 1890s all manner of sporting jewelry was popular. Besides horseshoes, which often carried the motto "Good luck," there were miniature riding crops, hunting horns, and fox heads for the huntress; silver bicycle pins for the cycling enthusiast; tennis racquet brooches for the tennis player; and a great deal of golf memorabilia. The sports of yachting, rowing, skating, and motoring were also celebrated by the 1890s silver brooch.

Sentimental brooches of the highest quality.

Victorians memorialized events with silver brooches, commemorating everything from the four seasons to state occasions, particularly Queen Victoria's two jubilees: her fiftieth, in 1887, and her sixtieth, in 1897. The last important silver commemorative brooches marked the death of England's beloved monarch in 1901.

A curious aspect of jewelry design in the late nineteenth century was the Victorian fascination with naughtiness. Bangle bracelets in the shape of corsets, with attendant laces and/or buttons, are rare but not impossible to find. These surprising and amusing pieces are sometimes referred to as Victorian pornographica, although they seem harmless enough by today's standards.

A collection of 1880s silver horseshoe brooches (facing page).

Silver corset bracelet, a Victorian curiosity.

N I E L L O

One must not overlook niello when enumerating the fashions in Victorian silver jewelry. Most popular in the last decade of the nineteenth century and previewing most appealingly the new look of the Art Nouveau era, niello (which comes from the Latin diminutive *nigellus*, meaning blackish) is a process in which a fusion of silver, copper, lead, and sulfur is melted and poured into designs incised on silver. The piece of jewelry was first fired in an oven called a muffle and then ground down and polished, the resulting surface taking on a most attractive gray metallic sheen. Often pink gold overlay was added to heighten the designs. A process that had been perfected centuries before in eastern Europe and Russia, Victorian niello work was done in France as well as in Russia, although a London-based firm, S. H. and D. Gass, exhibited niello bracelets at the Great Exhibition of 1851.

It is interesting to note that niello was usually made of a low-grade silver (marked 800) because it withstood firing better than the softer sterling. If there is gold work, it is either a low-karat pink gold or a gold wash over silver, depending on the fineness of a piece.

Niello bibelots in floral and grapevine patterns (facing page).

A group of French and Russian niello bracelets, c. 1890.

Niello chatelaine consisting of cigar cutter, stamp holder, needle case, manicure set, toothpick, pencil, knife, and whistle. Made in France, c. 1895 (left).

Closeup of intricate niello-work squirrel on the case of a small pocket watch (below).

Group of niello pocket watches and watch chains.

Niello work of the late 1880s and 1890s can be found in exquisitely simple geometric patterns of diamonds, squares, stripes, and fleur-de-lis or in lovely floral and grapevine designs. Russian niello work of the same period sometimes has a less tailored look, incorporating Cyrillic lettering into swirling chased designs. As the 1890s came to a close, niello work took on a decidedly Edwardian feeling: stars of pink gold on a dark gray metallic background. Although seen mostly on bracelets, brooches, and lockets, niello was not limited to ladies' jewelry: Watches, watch fobs, chatelaines, cuff links, stamp boxes, knives, and pens were made using this technique. Niello watch, muff, and guard chains exhibited a wide variety of fancy link work alternating plain silver, niello, and pink gold links that look extremely modern and are very wearable today.

Detail of flat-link niello chains (above).

Turn-of-the-century niello and pink gold watch with matching expansion band (right).

A collection of French niello lockets and chains (facing page).

53
≈

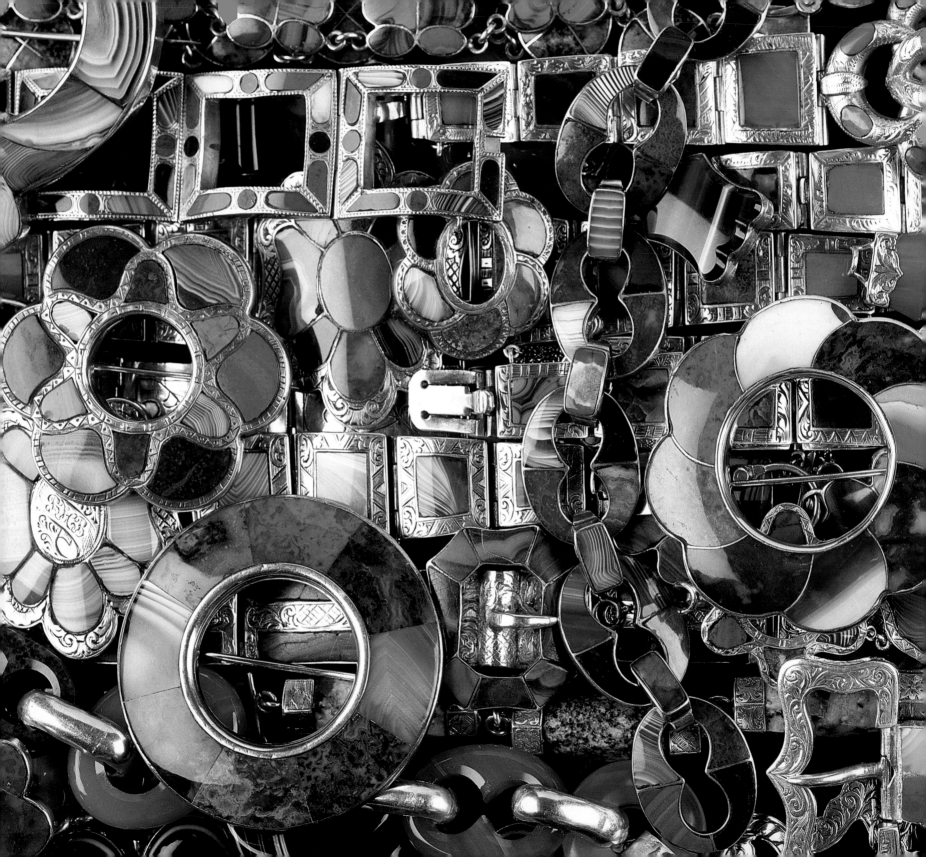

Stone

Scottish highland chiefs clad in their clan tartans.

Sovereign holder, matchbox, and pillbox set with colorful agates (facing page).

or almost a hundred and fifty years, Victorian agate jewelry has been called "Scottish agate" or "Scottish pebble jewelry." This is, in many cases, a misnomer, because a great deal of "Scottish agate" was made in England, not Scotland, often using stones that came from Germany rather than the British Isles.

However, the first jewelry to make use of attractive pebbles *was* produced in Scotland, and agate jewelry does owe its popularity to the unbridled enthusiasm for all things Scottish that swept England in the mid-1800s. The cultural climate in Victorian England was heightened by an awakening interest in naturalism and a renewed fascination with medieval romanticism. Picturesque Scotland became the embodiment

57
≈

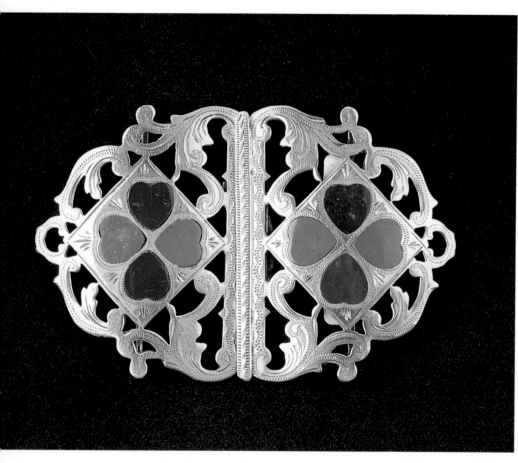

Silver belt buckle set with bloodstone and jasper in
the heart motif.

"St. Andrew's Cross" brooch made by G. & M.
Chrichton of Edinburgh.

of both, abetted by the writings of Sir Walter Scott that idealized the Scotsman, the visit of George IV to Scotland in full Highland regalia in 1822, and the purchase by Queen Victoria of Balmoral, her imposing Scottish castle, in 1847.

Victoria's love affair with Scotland was well publicized. She dressed her children in tartans and required all her guests to wear Scottish costumes to the Great Exhibition Ball of 1851. In her book *Leaves from the Journal of Our Life in the Highlands* she records her discovery of "cairngorms" (transparent orange-brown crystal quartz) when she ascended a mountain near Balmoral. With royal enthusiasm such as this, it was not long before Scotland became a major tourist attraction. Her loyal subjects traveled to Scotland to view the scenic wonders and experience a culture rich in tradition. As Highland dress had always been an intrinsic part of this culture and Scottish jewels an intrinsic part of Highland dress, it is no wonder that local jewelers, taking advantage of the increased tourist trade, began making jewelry for the traveler to bring-home to England. Most of it was made in Edinburgh, and it is estimated that by 1870 there were over a thousand people working in the Scottish jewelry trade. The souvenirs they crafted were indeed made of stones native to the hills and streams of Scotland, but as pebble jewelry became increasingly popular, in both England and France, England's foremost jewelry manufacturing center, Birmingham, began full-scale production of "Scottish" baubles.

Besides making traditional plaid brooches (circular brooches used to secure the Scotsman's shoulder tartan) and miniature dirks (dagger-shaped pins), Birmingham, bowing to the Victorian penchant for jewelry and bibelots of all sorts, made "Scottish" folk jewelry in non-traditional forms: bracelets, earrings, bar pins, pendants, necklaces (although only rarely), belt buckles, cuff links, stamp boxes, match safes, napkin rings, and sovereign holders.

In the 1860s, with business booming, Birmingham began a quest for new sources of agates and began importing quantities of nonindi-

Crescent-shaped agate brooch with cairngorm in star setting, mid-1800s.

genous stones from Germany, India, and Africa. Finally, Birmingham manufacturers began sending their silver mounts to Germany, where lapidaries selected, set, and polished the stones and returned the finished pieces to England. While there were still jewelers in Scotland turning out pebble jewelry, by the late 1800s the making of "Scottish agate" had indeed become an international business.

A detail of silver and banded-agate buckle bracelets.

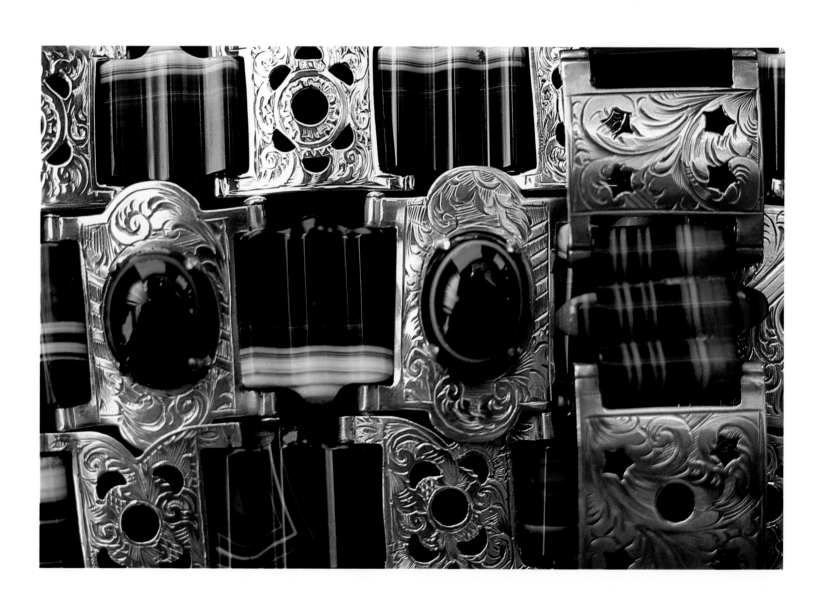

Granite bracelets from Aberdeen, c. 1800.

MATERIALS

Agate is a variety of quartz, a mineral composed of silicon dioxide. It can be clear and colorless or have variegated color arranged in layered stripes such as banded agate (usually black or brown and white) or Montrose agate (gray striated). It can have cloudlike or mosslike dendritic formations, as in moss agate (milky white agate with green inclusions) or mocha agate (brown inclusions). There are three distinct categories of quartz:

Transparent—crystalline stones such as amethysts (pale purple), citrines (pale yellow), and cairngorms (smoky orange brown).

Translucent—chalcedony (usually milky white or bluish), carnelian or cornelian (translucent red orange), and bloodstone (dark green with tiny red flecks).

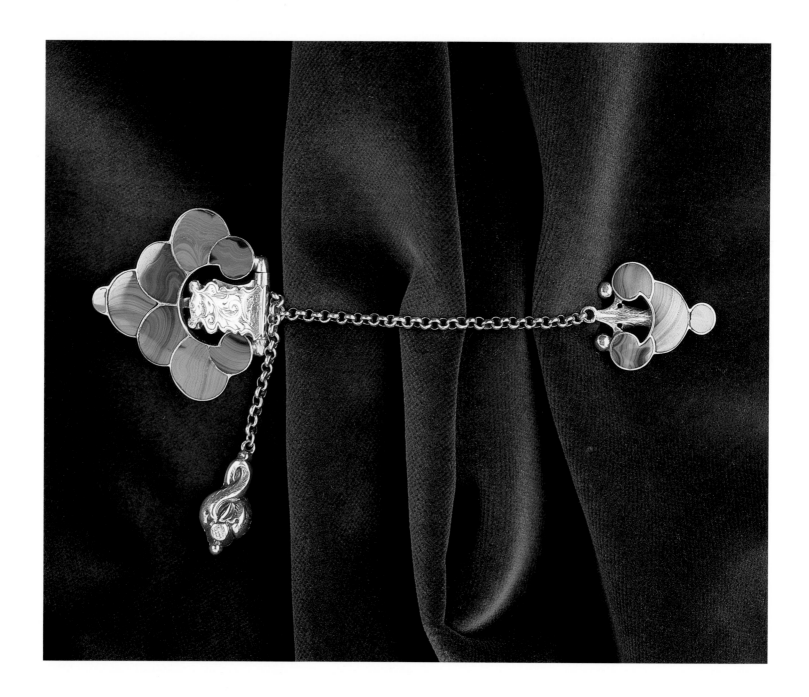

Handsome malachite cape pin, signed Bradford.

Opaque—jasper (usually red, mustard, or brown).

Another type of stone used in the making of agate jewelry was granite, a combination of quartz and microcline. Mined in Aberdeen, Scotland, it has a unique pink and gray coloring, and it was never mixed with other stones.

Malachite, a vivid green mineral composed of alternating bands of light and dark green, was in great demand by makers of agate jewelry. Found nowhere in Scotland, it was imported from Siberia by way of Germany.

M A N U F A C T U R E

Although it was possible that a talented craftsman could make an entire piece of agate jewelry, this required four different skills. More commonly, a silversmith would make the mount and pass that along to an engraver. It would then go to a stonecutter, who would shape and polish the agates and give everything to a jeweler, who would set the stones in the silver mount with pitch or shellac. Invisible once the stones were in place, the shellac would fill up most of the cavity and allow for shallower stones, causing a piece to be lighter in weight than it appeared. The color of the shellac was important since it affected the color of the more translucent stones it was supporting. In pieces of finer workmanship, stones were carefully chosen and subtly matched and cut to fit perfectly flush. The finished product was an artful mosaic indeed.

Makers of agate jewelry often created designs combining pebbles with citrines, amethysts, or cairngorms. Many of these stones were heat-treated and dyed to create more vivid colorings, and simulated citrines, amethysts, and cairngorms were sometimes used. In brooches, the pin backs were usually made of steel.

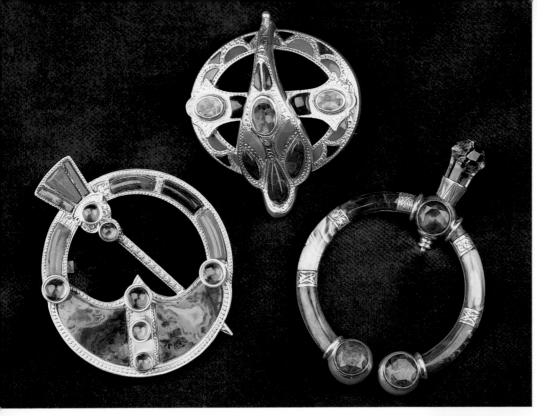

Mid-nineteenth-century agate brooches in
traditional Celtic motifs (left).

Agate brooches in variations of the star motif
(below).

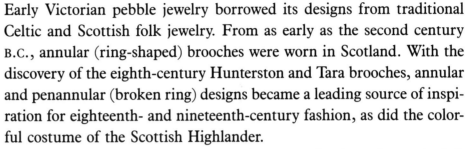

M O T I F S

Early Victorian pebble jewelry borrowed its designs from traditional Celtic and Scottish folk jewelry. From as early as the second century B.C., annular (ring-shaped) brooches were worn in Scotland. With the discovery of the eighth-century Hunterston and Tara brooches, annular and penannular (broken ring) designs became a leading source of inspiration for eighteenth- and nineteenth-century fashion, as did the colorful costume of the Scottish Highlander.

Highland dress required that a clan tartan be draped over the left shoulder and secured with a plaid brooch. These round target-shaped brooches numbered among the most popular designs of the early Victorian era, as did the "endless knot" (a Celtic motif), the "Cross of St. Andrew" (a diagonal cross that is a Scottish national emblem), and various shields, crests, and clan symbols.

A Scotsman's kilt was secured with a silver kilt pin. In imitation of the knives in jeweled scabbards that the Highlander sometimes wore, Victorian jewelers fashioned kilt pins to resemble miniature dirks replete with agates and cairngorms. The finest of these have diminutive knives that can be removed from their sheaths.

The heart was another traditional motif that maintained great popularity in the nineteenth century. One style of heart design characterized the luckenbooth, which depicts a heart, or two hearts entwined, surmounted by a crown. When the two entwined hearts are shaped like the letter "M," this is sometimes referred to as a Queen Mary brooch. Dating from the fourteenth century, luckenbooths were considered love tokens and protection against evil spirits.

The serpent was another symbol common to Victorian times, a particular favorite of Queen Victoria, whose betrothal ring was shaped

Illustration of a reproduction of the eighth-century Tara Brooch, from the catalog "Industry of All Nations," 1851.

like a serpent. Signifying eternity, the serpent was often depicted with a heart in its mouth, signifying love.

By the mid-Victorian years, traditional Scottish folk themes gave way to those current in England, such as the "buckled strap" that symbolized the Order of the Garter, which Queen Victoria headed. This became one of the most popular motifs in agate jewelry. Others played upon fashionable figural images of the day like anchors, arrows, stars, horseshoes, bows, leaves, butterflies, and seashells. One example of a particularly British motif is a marvelously detailed brooch in the shape of an umbrella.

Queen Mary luckenbooth of silver, agate, and enamel (above).

Intricately detailed umbrella brooch with British Registry mark on back, dated August 12, 1866 (left).

A group of brightly colored pebble brooches, the one on the right bearing the name of a city in Wales, Llandudno.

A collection of agate and silver dirks, one with a removable fruit knife (right).

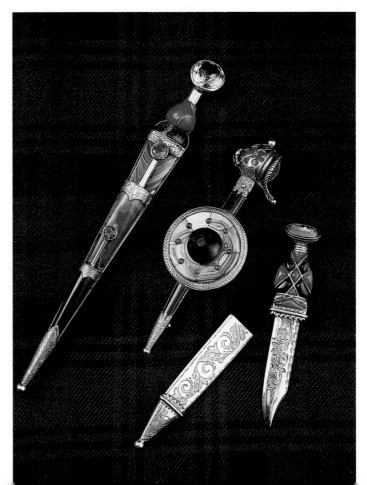

Exceptional mid-Victorian hinged snake bracelets.

Symbolic love-token brooches. Top: a luckenbooth; bottom: a serpent with a heart in its mouth, signifying eternal love (facing page).

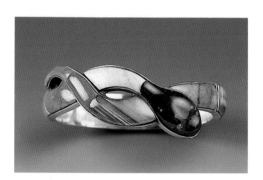

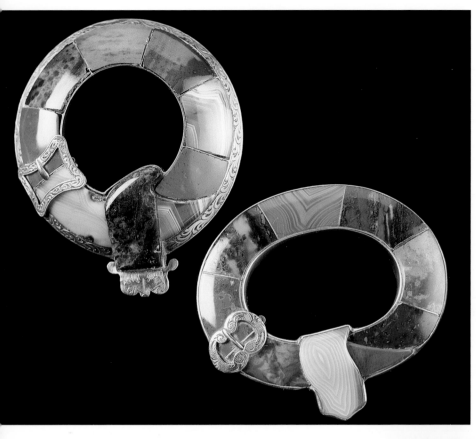

Buckled-strap brooches, signifying the Order of the Garter (left).

Hinged agate and silver bracelet with beautifully matched stones and floral center medallion, c. 1870 (below).

Agate brooch from Plymouth, England, ingeniously making use of striated agates to convey the feeling of a seashell (facing page).

A collection of agate anchor brooches (left).

Carnelian and silver arrow brooches (above).

Malachite "leaf" jewelry.

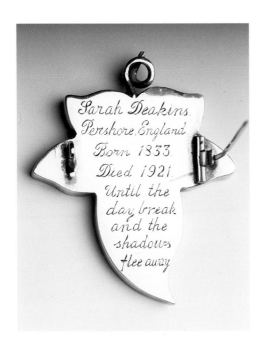

Sentimental inscription on the back of a malachite brooch, obviously inscribed after the departure of the loved one (left).

Strikingly modern-looking granite brooch and bracelet by M. Rettie and Sons of Aberdeen, mid-nineteenth century (facing page).

Agate "autumn leaves" bracelet in silver, and gold-mounted brooch with suspended leaf (below).

Signed granite heart-shaped brooch and earrings suite by Jamieson of Aberdeen (left).

Illustration from the catalog "Industry of All Nations," 1851 (right).

Messrs. RETTIE & SONS, of Aberdeen, exhibit some curious specimens of persevering ingenuity successfully exerted in a material the most unpromising. The hard and impracticable character of GRANITE would seem to defy delicacy and minutiæ of workmanship, and to preclude its becoming an article of personal decoration. Yet the BRACELETS here engraved are cut with much labour and patience from this material, the various parts being mounted and linked together in silver. A choice of granite has been made from Aberdeen, Balmoral, &c.; and, by dint of labour, a comparatively valueless article is elevated into the position of a precious stone, and placed among the fancy articles of a jewel case.

MAKERS

Although some agate jewelry made between 1842 and 1883 bears the diamond-shaped British Registry mark, little is known about its makers because very little of it was signed. However, through a study of individual pieces and the catalogs of the international exhibitions of 1851, 1862, and 1867, we know that the foremost makers were Muirhead of Glasgow; G. & M. Crichton, McKay and Cunningham, Marshall and Sons, and Meyer and Mortimer, all of Edinburgh; Jamieson and M. Rettie and Sons, both of Aberdeen; Bradford and Unite of Birmingham; and Ellis and Sons of Exeter. Of all these makers, only Chrichton, Bradford, Unite, Ellis, Rettie, and Jamieson consistently signed their jewelry. Although G. & M. Chrichton were primarily goldsmiths, the firm was known for fine silver and agate jewelry and spectacular citrine and amethyst plaid brooches. Ellis, Bradford, and Unite were known for their silver and pebble "safety-chain" brooches and cape pins. Both Rettie and Jamieson worked almost exclusively in pink and gray granite, mined locally in Aberdeen, and there are great sim-

A selection of brooches by Rettie, left, and Jamieson, right (right).

Rare mid-Victorian figural granite pin (below).

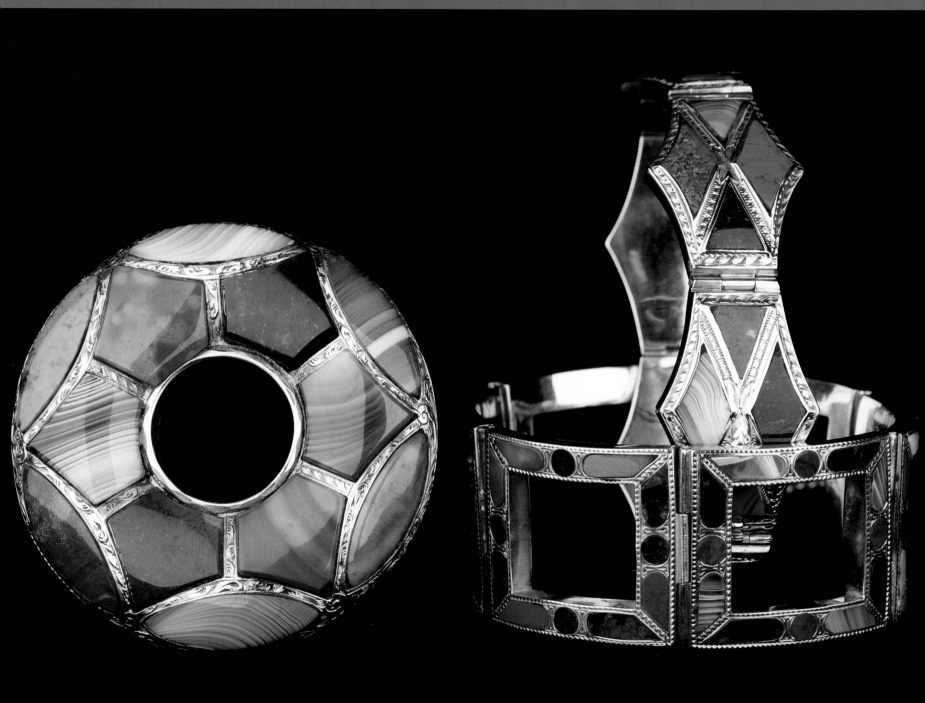

Heather-toned gold barrel bracelet, c. 1850, and agate circle pin set with citrines and amethysts.

Gold and agate jewelry of the finest quality, c. 1800 (facing page).

ilarities in their work. Extremely modern and geometric in feeling, brooches and bracelets by both these makers are clean of line, sparse of design, and immaculately set in silver, or sometimes gold, with little or no engraving. The stones are usually completely flush, and the pink Peterhead granite they used has a distinctive salmon-colored cast.

Pebble jewelry reached the height of its popularity as souvenir jewelry, some of it bearing the names of the places it was commemorating, such as Jersey (the Isle of), Llandudno (in Wales), and Aberdeen. Most souvenir agate was set in silver but there are rare and stunning pieces set in gold, indicating that it must have attracted even the extremely well-to-do. Needless to say, gold pebble jewelry is usually of the highest quality and finest workmanship. One of the earliest but most timeless designs in agate jewelry is the "barrel" bracelet: faceted agate cylinders set in silver or gold mounts that were popular in the late 1840s. Many early examples of pebble jewelry are slate-backed: mounted openly on slate with tiny silver or gold claws holding the agates in place. Historians believe these pieces are more likely to have been made in Scotland, and bracelets on display at the Hunterian Museum in Glasgow seem to support this idea.

The engraving on the silver mounts of pebble jewelry is done by hand and is usually elaborately Victorian in feeling. The most common designs are floral, foliate, and geometric. It is not unusual to see a different engraved pattern on each silver mount of an agate bracelet. In the last two decades of the century, the ornate engraving gave way to plain settings. Silver was used not only as a frame but sometimes as a thin demarcation between stones. Some pieces show no silver at all, just wonderfully sculpted stones set so perfectly it is hard to tell where one leaves off and the next begins. It is tempting to deduce that all work without engraving is of a later date, but that would not be quite accurate, as the 1850–60 work of Rettie and Jamieson attests.

As the industry moved to Birmingham, many pieces were die-cast and some bear Birmingham hallmarks. The quality of the work, however, did not necessarily decline; in fact, in some ways, it improved. Certainly there was a greater variety in style, color, and subject matter than ever before. Agate bracelets followed the prevailing fashions of the day with heavy hinged links and important center medallions sometimes crowned by an amethyst or citrine. Many had lovely padlock closures in the shape of hearts, shields, or locks, and "strap and buckle" belt bracelets were very popular. Dangling earrings were lightweight but well proportioned and followed the styles of the period. Figural themes took a turn to the whimsical with brooches in the shape of bagpipes, rowboats, tam-o'-shanters, and knights in armor.

Whimsical figural agate and silver brooches.

Agate brooches in variations of the bow motif (above).

Malachite padlock bracelet and brooch, possibly pieced and set in Germany (right).

From the beginning there had always been the natural affinity of bloodstone, jasper, and striated gray agate; carnelian and banded onyx; and the lovely soft combination of moss and heather, but Birmingham, searching for more unusual and exotic colorations, turned to Germany for stonework. One of the most nationalistic jewelry designs of the 1870s was a malachite bracelet bearing the symbols of three of the countries of the British Isles: the thistle for Scotland, the shamrock for Ireland, and the Tudor rose for England. It is somewhat ironic that this bracelet may well have been pieced, set, and polished in Idar-Oberstein, Germany!

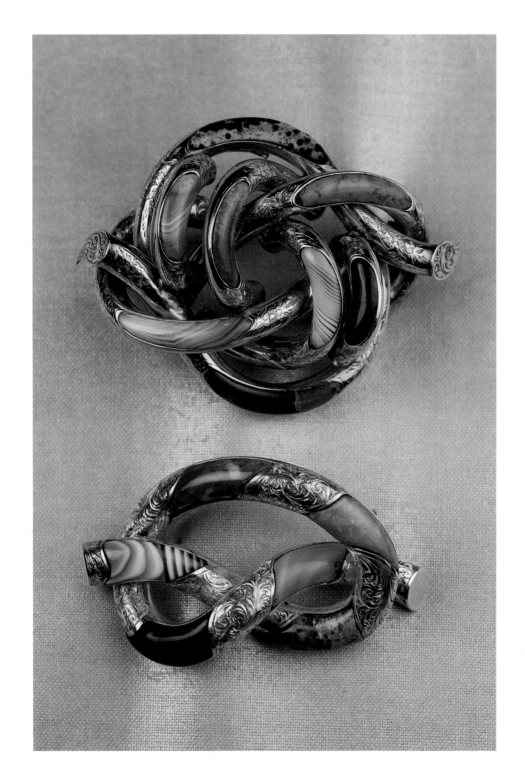

Gold and agate "knot" brooches.

Hinged agate bracelets with ornate center medallions, c. 1870 (facing page).

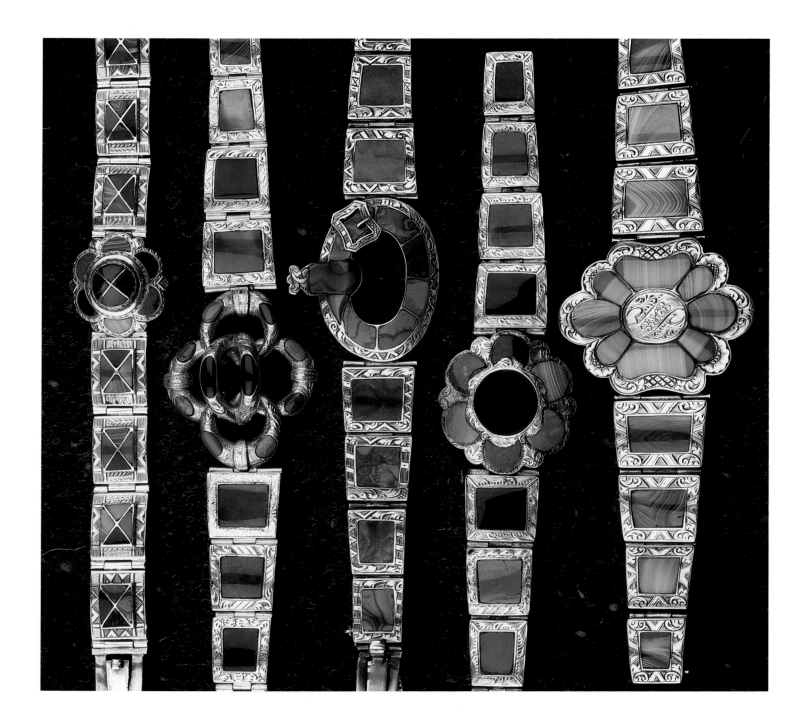

*Agate bracelets and brooches of beautifully
matched stones in shades of rose and mauve.*

*A collection of earrings in the classic shapes of the
mid-1800s (facing page).*

The antithesis of the soft and mutually complementary tones of most agates is the starkly striking black and white of banded onyx (a variety of banded agate). Naturally composed of parallel layers in varying shades of black, brown, and white, banded onyx is artificially colored by steeping it in a solution of honey and sulfuric acid; it is then heated so that carbon is released and the absorbent part is dyed black. This process enhances both the layered structure of the stone and the contrast in coloration.

Link bracelet with exceptionally fine padlock containing a hair compartment, and brooches in matching colorations.

Unusual locket-top hinged agate bracelet enclosing a photograph of a Victorian gentleman.

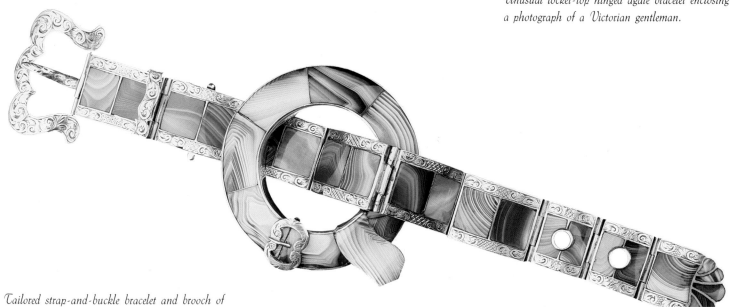

Tailored strap-and-buckle bracelet and brooch of striated gray agate.

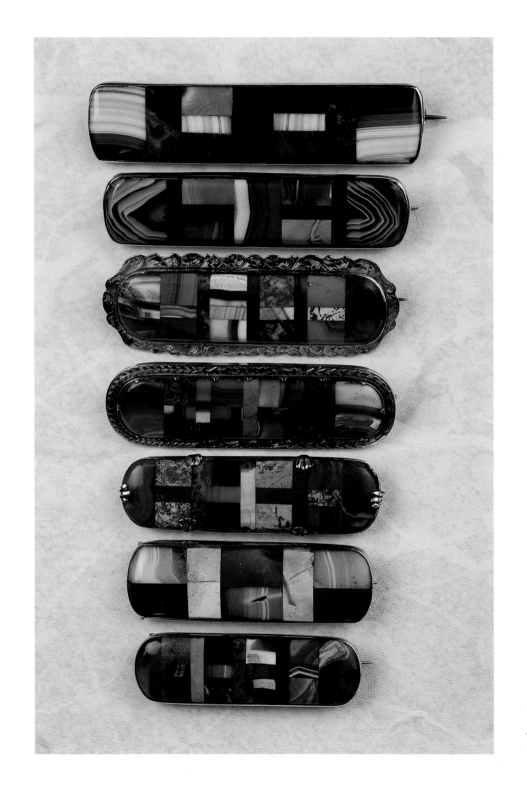

A collection of "plaid" bar pins.

Agate brooches of the finest workmanship, c. 1880 (facing page).

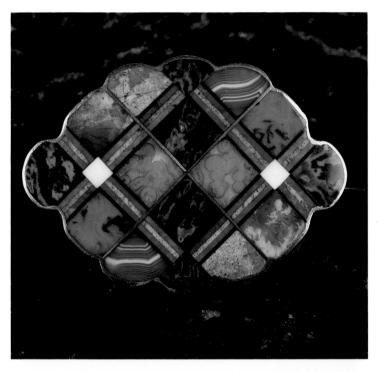

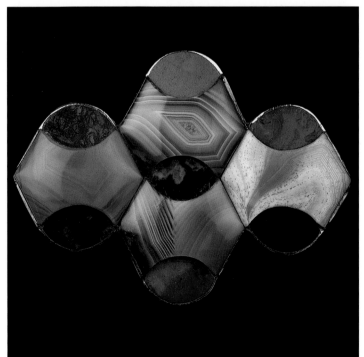

Target brooches: The one on the left is in a cut-steel frame, and the two on the right incorporate the St. Andrew's Cross design.

Banded-agate and gold bracelet with matching earrings, c. 1860 (facing page).

Finally, one cannot overlook the impact that agate jewelry had on fashion throughout the entire Victorian era. *Englishwoman's Domestic Magazine* in 1867 had this to say: "Scotch jewelry as well as Scotch costume is *de rigueur* and the badges of the different clans are worn as brooches, earrings, buckles and shoe rosettes." *The Paris Exhibition of 1878: An Illustrated Weekly Review* reported the Scottish image still very much in fashion: "Is it possible to find anywhere . . . a prouder, more gorgeous spectacle than that of a Highland piper in full national costume? . . . the clan-tartan enhanced by a multitude of engraved silver buttons, shoulder brooches, embossed buckles, jeweled dirks . . . a perfectly dazzling combination of silver combined with precious stones."

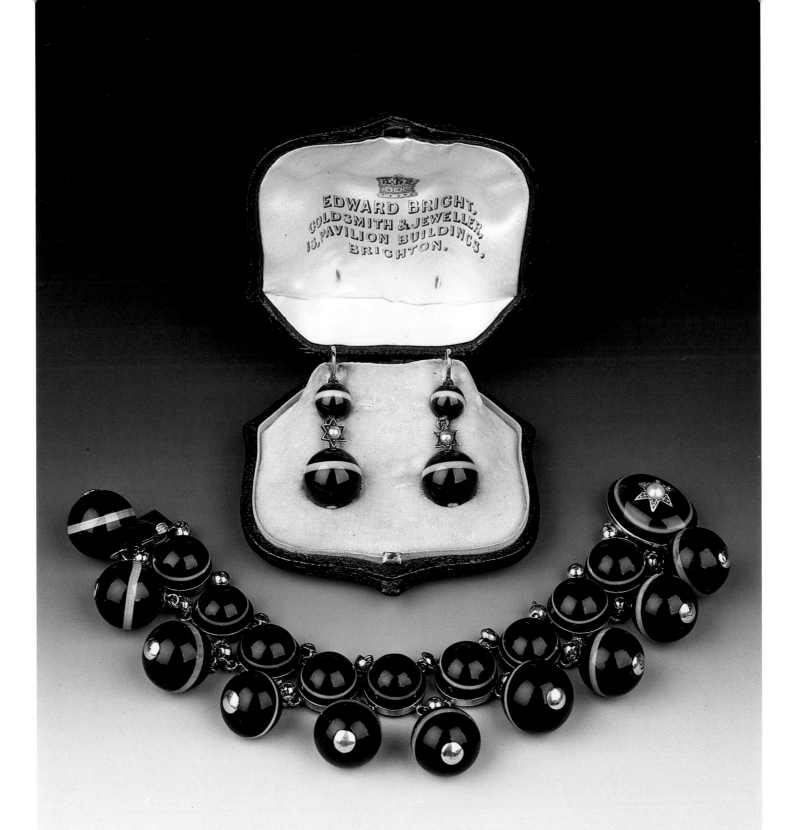

Banded-agate necklace and cross with a remarkable cross-shaped inclusion in the stone.

Banded-agate brooches, c. 1880.

"Ribbon" brooch with interesting striations in banded agate (right).

Although its popularity declined from the beginning of World War I to the end of World War II, there was still an abundance of pebble jewelry produced well into the twentieth century, but the consensus of opinion is that most of it has neither the quality nor the magic of Victorian agate.

Outstanding silver and agate bracelet of hinged seashell shapes, and circle brooch with agates pieced to spell "*REGARD*" (left).

Modified Tara Brooch set with cairngorms, and bangle bracelet set with agates, citrines, and amethyst (below).

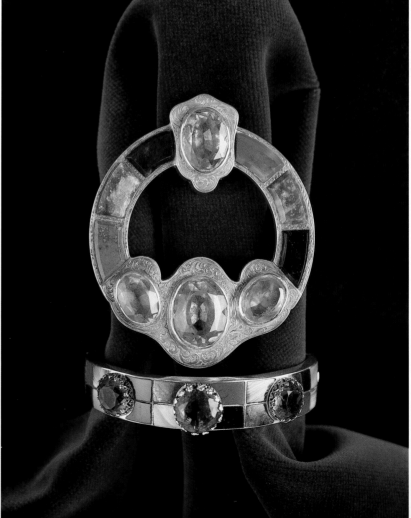

Rare oversized gold and agate Scottish dirk.

Steel

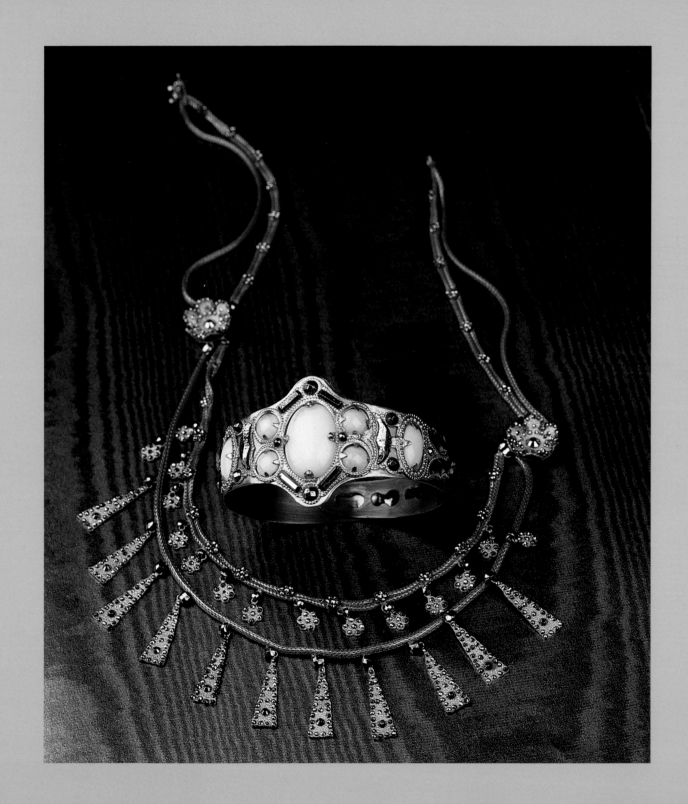

French cut-steel and gilt-metal fringed necklace and gilt-metal bracelet set with cut steel and paste opals.

*A*mid the delicate precious-stone and gold work of the Victorian era, nothing stands out quite as surprisingly as the jewelry made of unusual metals such as steel, iron, gunmetal, and aluminum. Cut steel and Berlin iron both owe their origins to the eighteenth century but continued to be in vogue up to the mid-nineteenth. These two metals had a somewhat historical significance in both France and Germany: Jewelry made of them was worn by noblemen who had donated their precious jewels to their country. Gunmetal and aluminum, however, belong to the latter half of the nineteenth century and were a Victorian paradox: a most romantic effect from some of the least poetic materials ever used in jewelry making.

Detail of flexible cut-steel bracelet, showing the riveted underside.

C U T   S T E E L

Although steel work is said to date back possibly to Elizabethan times, it first became a lucrative cottage industry in the mid-eighteenth century. This industry was situated in the little Oxfordshire town of Woodstock and specialized in the making of steel "toys," a term for trinkets and jewelry such as chatelaines, watch chains, scissors, and sword hilts. As the demand for cut-steel jewelry grew in both England and France, Birmingham, under the supervision of industrialist Matthew Boulton, began manufacturing quantities of cut-steel buttons and jewelry in the late 1700s. By using women as cheap labor, Birmingham eventually overshadowed Woodstock and continued to be the primary source of cut steel until it went out of style in the last quarter of the 1800s. Although no one seems to know how much jewelry was made in Woodstock, it is generally believed that Woodstock's work was superior to Birmingham's; it was certainly more expensive. There is a record of a pair of steel scissors costing fifteen guineas (British gold coins worth over one pound each) in 1778!

The most important object that the new industry produced was that relic of masculine vanity, the cut-steel shoe buckle. Even now, it is the item one sees most often. When the shoe buckle went out of fashion at the end of the eighteenth century, the industry went into a decline until the demand for cut-steel jewelry revived it.

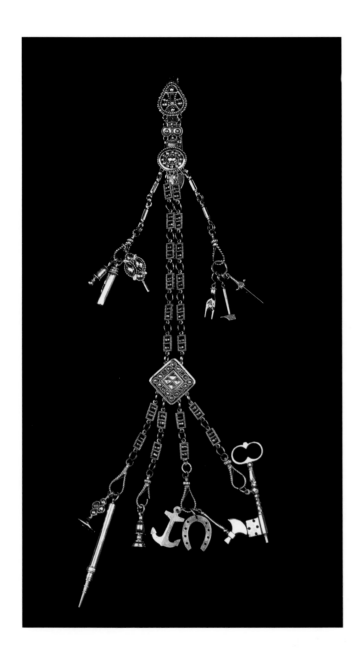

Eighteenth-century French cut-steel chatelaine (left).

Group of cut-steel trinkets: shoe buckles, belt buckle, buttons, heel ornaments, and cape clasp (below).

Cut-steel jewelry is comprised of tiny nails or studs mounted into base plates. It has been said that the earliest source for this material was the horseshoe nails that littered the streets of the enterprising towns of Woodstock, Wolverhampton, and Salisbury, but surely, after cut steel became a lucrative business, this random source of soft steel could not have been its major one.

Making cut-steel jewelry was difficult and time-consuming. First, the steel nails or studs were individually faceted and polished. (The best early pieces had as many as fifteen facets, whereas most Victorian pieces had five.) Then they were riveted one at a time through tiny holes in a base plate usually made of brass or low-grade silver. The studs were

Hard bangle and flexible cut-steel bracelets, c. 1830.

Mid-Victorian cut-steel fringed necklace and earrings using the star motif.

faceted and mounted in such a way as to catch as much light as possible and provide a brilliance not unlike that of diamonds. Very ornate examples had more than one base plate to give the piece dimension; these plates were affixed to each other by tiny steel supports on the underside. If a piece had a center medallion, it was usually mobile. One can distinguish the pieces that are made of individual studs simply by turning them over and noticing the rivets' lack of uniformity. Later, the mass production of cut steel—in which studs were stamped out in ribbonlike sheets rather than individually riveted—caused its decline. In top quality cut-steel jewelry, one sees the use of a variety of different-sized studs to create a more brilliant effect. Often, large studs are surrounded by rings of smaller ones.

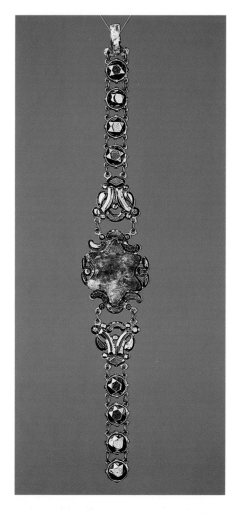

Early-nineteenth-century cut-steel bracelet with moss agate center medallion (left).

Late-nineteenth-century cut-steel earrings with moonstone drops, marked France.

In necklaces, the finer pieces have graduated drops, stars, or rosettes rather than uniform ones. While most brooches were made of densely packed studs, some have naturalistic designs in which the studs are arranged spatially to produce delicate floral sprays. The most desirable cut-steel brooches are those supporting *pampilles* (dangling cas-

cades of graduated drops) in imitation of the fine diamond jewelry of the period.

Although cut steel was never signed, it is possible to date pieces by their subject matter, since the same themes that were fashionable in precious jewelry prevailed in cut steel. Because the shoe buckle declined in the late 1700s one can assume that most cut-steel shoe buckles date from prior to this period, as do many other trinkets such as chatelaines. However, Anne Clifford, noted expert on cut steel, believes that, contrary to popular opinion, most of the cut-steel jewelry that has survived today was made in the mid-1800s, not earlier. Early-nineteenth-century pieces are usually naturalistic, mostly in floral rosette designs. Most figural pieces are mid-nineteenth century, such as anchors, hearts, lizards, bees, butterflies, keys, moons, and stars. Bracelets came in two varieties: hard bangles (which are more common) and finer, flexible ones. Among the other types of jewelry made were pendants, earrings with cut-steel "fringe," belt buckles, tiaras, hair combs, and buttons.

Unusual but not unobtainable today are pieces that combine cut steel with other materials such as pinchbeck, jet, Wedgwood, enamel, and river pearls. Often these pieces are backed with mother-of-pearl for a more luxurious feeling against the skin. Sequins, or paillettes, were also made of cut steel, and lovely eighteenth-century steel mesh bracelets adorned with paillettes are prized today. Of lasting appeal are superb cut-steel chains such as Matthew Boulton made for Queen Charlotte in 1767. They were extremely costly, fashioned of thin, beautifully polished cut-steel slices in circular and floret shapes.

Cut steel was just as popular in France as it was in England, dating from 1759 when wealthy people, who were asked to donate their jewels to the treasury, began wearing cut steel instead. Much of what Birmingham made in the mid-1700s was exported to France until a Yorkshireman named Sykes moved to Paris in 1780 and began a cut-steel industry there. By the late eighteenth century, cut steel had become big business, and Frenchmen such as Deferney, Dauffe, and Frichot all had thriving enterprises. Frichot was best known for his huge parures in floral motifs. Even Napoleon was not blind to the brilliance of cut steel: He bought Empress Marie Louise an impressive parure from Deferney. A most celebrated Parisian boutique was Au Petit Dunkerque, owned by a Monsieur Granchez, Marie Antoinette's jeweler. It was here that jewelry made of cut steel sold for a higher price than gold.

Cut steel combined well with agates, such as moss agate and carnelian, and other semiprecious stones. Some fine-quality French pieces using moonstones and citrines were made at the end of the nineteenth century and marked "France," but for the most part the cut steel made in the last quarter of the century in France and in England was of poor quality and little consequence, with the exception of the jewelry made by the W. Hipkins Co. of Birmingham.

Selection of unriveted polished-steel jewelry.

It is hard to find great examples of cut-steel jewelry today because much of it has succumbed to a cruel fate: rust in the face of dampness. But when they appear, they are prized by most collectors of Victorian jewelry. This was not always so. Jewelry historian Joan Evans, in her 1953 classic *A History of Jewellery, 1100–1870* echoed a sentiment that was shared by other experts: "Such jewellery [cut steel] remains the nadir to which the jeweller's art sank in the century that saw the dawn of the Industrial Revolution."

A fascinating offshoot of cut-steel jewelry is the type that is not riveted but is, in and of itself, made from polished and faceted steel. These pieces do not mimic precious jewels but are rather striking and strong in a no-nonsense way, revealing that steel in its own right can be a beautiful adornment.

Cut steel is often confused with marcasite jewelry because both possess a similar gray metallic sheen, but marcasites are made of iron pyrites that are set in prongs, like diamonds, and are never riveted.

BERLIN IRON

Although most Berlin iron jewelry was produced before 1837, it must be included in any book focusing on Victorian jewelry made of unusual materials. It is believed that the process of making this black-lacquered cast-iron jewelry originated with the Gleiwitz Foundry in Silesia, Prussia, in the late 1790s, but was taken up shortly thereafter by the Royal Berlin Foundry in Berlin in 1804. French production of iron jewelry, it is thought, began two years later, when Napoleon marched on Berlin, confiscated the casting molds, and brought them back to France. Berlin iron did not gain international attention, however, until the end of the Napoleonic Wars (1813–15), when Germany asked its wealthy to contribute their precious jewels to the war effort and gave its patrons, in return, iron jewelry that bore the inscription *"Gold gab ich für Eisen 1813"* (I gave gold for iron). It is ironic that the very jewelry Napoleon had so valued thus contributed to his downfall. Berlin iron's popularity did not end with the war. Its unique style had an appeal throughout Europe, and it was considered very desirable as mourning jewelry in France, England, and Germany.

Berlin iron was made by molding shapes in wax, impressing these shapes in a fine sand, and then filling the impression with molten iron. The cast pieces were left to cool, finished by hand, and lacquered black.

Berlin iron cross embellished with cut-steel stars, c. 1820.

The most common examples of this jewelry are parures (suites of necklaces, pairs of bracelets, brooches, and earrings) as well as rings, combs, and fans. It is not unusual to see Berlin iron crosses, as thousands of these were produced to commemorate the death of Queen Luisa of Prussia.

Berlin iron jewelry seems to have undergone three distinct transitions in design. The earliest pieces were strictly of the neoclassic school: medallions and cameos portraying classical figures linked by chains of iron mesh. From 1815 on, there was a shift toward realism, and designs are leafy, floral, and naturalistic. From 1830 to 1850, the trend in Berlin iron jewelry was toward Gothic Revival, and many of the pieces look like ornate miniature wrought-iron gates.

Although most Berlin ironwork is not signed, it becomes much more historically significant when it is. The most famous foundries that signed their work were Geiss, Lehmann, Schott, Hossauer, and Devaranne of Berlin. Some Berlin iron is enhanced by gold work, and these pieces are particularly desirable. The most important designer of Berlin iron jewelry was Karl Schinkel, who worked for the Berlin foundries and is said to have developed the Gothic Revival style that suits Berlin iron so perfectly.

Of particular beauty is the jewelry made of very fine strands of black or blue-gray wire mesh and thought to have been produced by the earliest iron foundry in Silesia. However, opinion of late is that much iron-mesh work was made in England and France, and the contrast in color and design between Berlin iron and most "Silesian wire" lends credence to this. Wire jewelry runs the gamut from work that is extremely fine and delicate, often ornamented with brilliant cut-steel paillettes, to heavier wire pieces that bear an uncanny resemblance to Brillo pads!

Berlin iron, too, was made in varying degrees of quality, and the consensus is that most post-1850 pieces lack the workmanship of the earlier years.

Berlin iron bracelet, earrings, and brooch in the Gothic Revival style, c. 1840. The bracelet is signed "A. F. Lehman—Berlin" (above).

Silesian-wire bracelet, earrings, and brooch, c. 1845 (right).

Oversized Berlin iron earrings, four inches long, c. 1830 (facing page).

Silesian-wire necklace and bracelet of the highest quality, c. 1830.

Silesian-wire "Brillo" necklace and bracelet.

ALUMINUM

In the mid-1800s, aluminum jewelry made a brief but unforgettable appearance. Aluminum, a very lightweight, silver-white metal, was discovered in 1827 and for the next few decades was prized more highly than gold. It was a metal so rare and an object of such curiosity, in fact, that in the 1850s jewelers in France, such as H. Bourdoncle, began using it experimentally in combination with high-karat gold for the creation of wonderful parures of Gothic architectural design. They were fascinated by its light weight and delighted by the fact that it did not oxidize as did silver.

Gothic Revival aluminum and gilt-metal bracelet and hatpins, c. 1800.

Aluminum jewelry first made its appearance at the Great Exhibition of 1851, but it was at the Exhibition of 1867 that it really caused a stir. It was considered so desirable that both Queen Victoria and Empress Marie Louise owned suites of aluminum and gold jewelry.

When it was not offset by gold, aluminum was often offset beautifully by gilt metal with a yellow or pink gold tinge. Pieces by Parisian jeweler Charles Henry Villemon, dating from 1860, are especially lovely, with bright hammered engravings in quatrefoil leaf motifs.

It is extremely difficult to find Victorian aluminum jewelry today, but when you do come across it, it is always exquisitely made and usually shockingly expensive. One sees, from time to time, bracelets with dangling drops, brooches, earrings, and shirt studs. Necklaces are extremely rare. The aluminum is almost always embellished by gilt metal or gold.

By the end of the nineteenth century, aluminum was mass produced in large commercial quantities, and because it was no longer prized for its rarity, aluminum jewelry disappeared.

Unique gunmetal wristwatch, late nineteenth century (facing page).

Matching bracelet and brooch of gilt metal and aluminum, using the quatrefoil leaf motif, c. 1860.

G U N M E T A L

Toward the end of the nineteenth century, another unusual metal for jewelry made its appearance: gunmetal. Although originally made of bronze, and then of an alloy of copper and tin, by the end of the century gunmetal was often made of iron, and the term was applied to any metal with that distinctive mat black color and smooth silky finish. Gunmetal probably became popular as an alternative to such other dark materials for mourning jewelry as jet, tortoiseshell, and gutta-percha. While gunmetal's ancestor was most certainly Berlin iron, its look was decidedly different. Gone were the Gothic curlicues and wrought-iron-gate look, replaced by the ultramodern, elegant, and simple blue-black jewelry that is still so wearable today.

Gunmetal seems mostly to have been made in France, Austria, and Germany, but it was also made at the turn of the century in New York by companies such as Ketcham and McDougall, who did a sizable business in watch fobs, chains, and pins and signed their work.

Gunmetal jewelry is still quite easy to find and not overpriced. One most often sees decorative chains that came in varying lengths for varying purposes: watch chains, chatelaine chains, muff chains, guard chains, and so on. The black links are often interspersed with tiny colored crystals, gold or steel balls, or iron filigree work. Especially charming are the lovely mesh purses that turn-of-the-century ladies attached to their belts or chatelaines. Chatelaines were often outfitted with pencil, pad, key, manicure and sewing kits, and powder box.

Match safes and other bibelots are sometimes set with tiny turquoises or amethysts to enliven the dull black finish. It is unusual to see bracelets or earrings made of gunmetal, but you can still find lovely lockets, some of them heart-shaped, distinguished-looking watch fobs, pocket watches, and wristwatches.

Gunmetal chatelaine with notepad, powder puff, sovereign holder, and change purse (left).

An array of gunmetal chains, fobs, and trinkets, late 1800s (below).

Cascade of metal chains: (left to right) polished steel, Berlin iron, cut steel, Silesian wire, and gunmetal.

Sentiment

Exceptionally large Whitby jet snake necklace and brooch.

f only one category of Victorian jewelry could be used to define the feeling of the nineteenth century, it would have to be the jewelry of sentiment. Sentimental jewelry was made from all sorts of materials, engineered in all sorts of ways, and inspired by all sorts of fashion influences. What unified it all was the use as its central image of the themes of love and remembrance. It employed all the classic symbols: the heart, the outstretched hand, clasped hands, angels, Cupid, the serpent, and the endless knot. It knew no social bounds because, with the advent of industrial mechanization and less expensive materials, sentimental jewelry was within the reach of just about everyone.

While much sentimental jewelry was worn to honor the dead in accordance with the strict mourning codes of Victoria's reign, just as much of it was worn for betrothal, love, and friendship. Materials such as jet were originally intended for mourning, but noteworthy people, such as Victorian opera singer Adelina Patti, made jet a desirable fashion accessory whether one was in mourning or not. Hair jewelry began as memento mori (mourning jewelry) in the eighteenth century, but by the mid-nineteenth just as many people were wearing the hair of their living loved ones.

This is not to say that mourning did not play a large part in the lives of the Victorians. Victoria's own stringent code of mourning for her beloved consort, Prince Albert, was emulated by her loyal subjects, and between royal deaths and their own personal tragedies (which were

Photograph of opera singer Adelina Patti bedecked in her jet finery.

Faceted Whitby jet snake bracelets, c. 1870 (left).

The Whitby jet factory of William Wright of Hagersgate, c. 1875 (facing page).

many in those medically more primitive times), mourning was, for many, a way of life with complex rules and regulations. After a period of full mourning (usually six months to a year), there was often a period of half-mourning in which the mourning code was slightly relaxed. Jewelry, when worn, had to comply with this code. In Queen Victoria's court following Albert's death only jet was permitted to be worn. The upper classes seemed to favor pieces made of black enamel on gold or onyx. All classes—upper, middle, and working—wore jet, but where it was too expensive cheaper substitutes such as French jet, gutta-percha, and bog oak were used. For half-mourning, tortoiseshell and tortoiseshell piqué as well as niello and studded gunmetal were deemed appropriate.

JET

Jet is a coal-like, carbonized black substance formed by heat, pressure, and a chemical reaction on ancient driftwood. It is said to have been used during the Bronze Age for small personal articles and again during the Roman era. In medieval England, monks in monasteries used jet to fashion rosary beads and crosses. But it really came into its own during the nineteenth century when a little town on the Yorkshire coast called Whitby began mining the jet from its cliffs and turning out mourning jewelry for all of England and Europe. Whitby began the manufacture of jet jewelry in the 1830s, came into world prominence with the Great Exhibition of 1851, grew to heroic proportions after the death of Prince Albert in 1861, and by 1870 counted over fourteen hundred workers in one hundred shops turning out a massive amount of jet mourning jewelry.

Whitby's jet carvers worked long, arduous hours under grueling conditions. The jet was worked on a lathe and then carved, some of it by hand, and finally polished on a series of wheels. Women workers did the

finishing, which involved assembling and stringing the work. Many of the workers were specialists who did only certain parts of the job: turning beads, carving chains, engraving floral designs, or making cameos.

Jet is extremely lightweight, but the jewelry made from it is astonishingly powerful looking. The Whitby industry specialized in elaborately carved beaded necklaces and chains, some of which were made from a single piece of jet. Often there were pendants or lockets suspended from the links. Bracelets, which were often sold in pairs, were usually strung on elastic or, in the case of the extremely popular snake bracelets, on wire. Earrings could be quite large because of jet's light weight, and brooches, too, were oversized, some of them measuring more than three inches in diameter. The most desirable brooches are not only large but have movable parts: dangling chains, tassels, or spheres. Padlock bracelets were made from large jet cable links with closures shaped like hearts or locks. The technique of faceting the jet to give it more reflective surfaces was widely practiced. Jet combined effectively with other materials such as shell cameos, cut-steel studs, silver buckles, even aluminum.

Unfortunately, most jet craftsmen rarely signed their work, but we do know who some of the great makers were. The most famous of them all was E. H. Greenbury, who won the Freedom Medal of the Worshipful Company of Turners. In 1854 he received a request from the queen of Bavaria for a giant jet chain, over four feet long. H. Barraclough was known for his carvings of flowers and fruit, and other well-known makers included W. H. Crane, Thomas Jose, T. Kraggs, and W. Lund.

By the 1880s, the jet industry had declined. Partly because the nation was tired of mourning, and partly because "French jet" and other cheaper jet substitutes had substantially encroached on the market, by 1884 there were only three hundred workers turning out jet in Whitby. In 1887, with the approach of her Silver Jubilee, Queen Victo-

Two Whitby jet brooches of considerable proportions, with movable parts.

Mourning earrings in the styles of the day, c. 1880: (top to bottom) jet, gutta-percha, jet (facing page).

ria at last relaxed her mourning code and sealed the fate of the Whitby jet industry.

Some of the imitations of jet, such as "French jet," were used to dramatic effect. French jet is not fossilized wood but black glass backed with lead. Because it was not as fragile as Whitby jet, it was used for making pieces of more intricate construction and greater delicacy. Especially effective are the ornate earrings and brooches in the shape of tiny flowers, hearts, or stars all connected by "invisible" wire on the underside. Unlike Whitby jet, it is very brittle and cold to the touch.

Whitby jet "endless knot" brooches (left).

Pair of Whitby jet expansion bracelets with ornamental silver buckles (below).

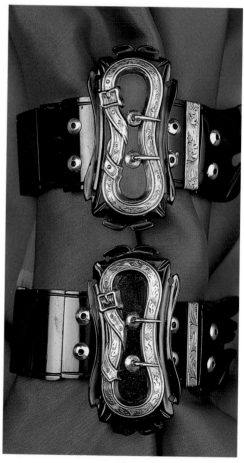

"Stretchy" jet bracelets (facing page, left).

Tortoiseshell, gutta-percha, and bog oak bracelets with gold trim, c. 1885 (facing page, right).

Bog oak was another substitute for jet, although more of a nationalistic than an economic one. A dark brown fossilized material that came from the peat bogs of Ireland, it was particularly popular in the 1850s and was usually carved into shamrocks, harps, castles, and other Celtic motifs. Bog oak was also a wonderful material for romantic carved and beaded necklaces and earrings.

The most interesting substitute for jet was a composition rubber called gutta-percha, also known as vulcanite. Unlike jet and bog oak, which were worked by carving, gutta-percha was molded and mass-produced to convincing effect in many of the same styles as jet and bog oak. It is a hard black substance that smells like rubber when it is rubbed and turns brown when exposed to sunlight for long periods of time. It was often used in the making of chains and bangles, and frequently embellished with brass or gold trim. Its mat finish was combined attractively with glossy jet trim for earrings, brooches, and bracelets.

Bog oak brooch and earrings suite on original card (above).

Bog oak necklace (right).

Exquisite French jet earrings (left).

Tortoiseshell padlock bracelet embellished with a silver keyhole.

Mid-Victorian tortoiseshell locket and matching bangle bracelets with cameos (facing page).

TORTOISESHELL AND PIQUE

The Victorians were very fond of tortoiseshell and used it for hair ornaments, combs, brushes, fans, and small boxes as well as jewelry. It was considered appropriate for mourning. Tortoiseshell did not come from the tortoise but, rather, from the hawksbill turtle found off the coasts of the West Indies and South America. The best color of tortoise-shell is considered to be dark brown with translucent yellow mottlings; it is found on the overlapping plates covering the carapace (upper shell) of the turtle. Light amber-yellow tortoiseshell comes from the plates on the underside and is known as "yellow belly" tortoiseshell.

Tortoiseshell is molded using heat and then polished. Although it was quite expensive, it was extremely popular in the 1830s and 1840s when a return to naturalism inspired the making of tortoiseshell accessories in the shape of twigs and branches. Most common in jewelry were the lustrous-feeling heavy chains and lockets, sometimes with cameos, and the earring and brooch sets often shaped like classical Greek urns.

The technique of inlaying gold and silver into tortoiseshell is called piqué, and it was introduced in England by refugee Huguenot craftsmen in the seventeenth century. It was first used for small decorative objects, but by the mid-nineteenth century there was a large trade making piqué jewelry by hand.

There were two different styles of piqué work: piqué point and pique posé. Piqué point refers to the tortoiseshell jewelry inlaid with patterns of tiny dots, stars, and diamonds made by pushing thin wires into the tortoiseshell and then filing them flush with the surface. Piqué posé is the technique of using strips of gold or silver sheet metal in

Collection of tortoiseshell and gutta-percha bangles with gold inlay, c. 1880.

floral, geometric, and scalloped designs and impressing them into the warmed and softened tortoiseshell. A combination of both piqué point and piqué posé is sometimes found on the same piece of jewelry. While each of these techniques creates a very different effect, they are both beautiful to behold.

Beads, bangles, hat pins, buttons, and belt buckles were among the trinkets made of piqué, but most impressive were the earrings that followed the fashions of the day in torpedo and pendulum shapes, hooped Creole-style ovals and dangling balls glittering with gold stars. Figural brooches in the shape of birds and butterflies are especially pleasing.

By the 1860s, piqué was at the height of its popularity, but in the 1870s Birmingham discovered a way to mass-produce it and the quality quickly deteriorated. It is easy to tell the machine-made pieces from the handmade ones because the stamped-out designs are unwaveringly uniform and one-dimensional in feeling.

Piqué heart charm on a gutta-percha and gold chain (above).

Mid-Victorian tortoiseshell bracelet employing the techniques of piqué posé and piqué point (right).

Piqué earrings in pendulum, ball, torpedo, and oval shapes, c. 1860 (above).

Delicate mid-nineteenth-century tortoiseshell brooch with drops (right).

Three mid-nineteenth-century piqué brooches and oversized earrings (facing page).

Today, the tortoise is an endangered species, and there are laws in the United States forbidding its slaughter. It might be suggested that Victorian tortoiseshell and piqué are also endangered species, fast disappearing from the antiques world and never to be replaced or made again.

Oversized piqué earrings and necklace (possibly assembled from Victorian notions).

Varieties of braided or woven hair bracelets set in gold, c. 1883 (right).

Late Victorian openwork hair brooch and figural charms made into earrings (below).

H A I R

"Whose hair I wear, I loved most dear" is an old epigram that explains, as much as anything can, the inexplicable fad of hair jewelry—adornments made from a loved one's lock of hair.

The popularity of hair jewelry began in the seventeenth century with the custom of distributing mourning rings containing the deceased's hair and grew in the eighteenth century to include rings and brooches that incorporated little vignettes under glass in the neoclassical style of the day: a tombstone, a swooning maiden, and a weeping willow tree in which the leaves were actually made of the loved one's hair. Almost all mourning jewelry from that time forward bore a small compartment in which to enshrine a lock of hair. It is interesting to note that what might seem morbid to us in the twentieth century was embraced wholeheartedly throughout the eighteenth and nineteenth centuries.

Except for a brief period in 1838 when, for some reason, hair jewelry was reviled, it enjoyed a popularity right up to the last quarter of the century. At its height, hair jewelry was used to commemorate betrothals and weddings as well as deaths and was made in a fantastic variety of shapes, sizes, and items.

Once again, it was to Victoria that credit (or blame) could be given for nineteenth-century England's fascination with hair jewelry. On her sixteenth birthday, her mother presented her with a brooch made of her (mother's) hair, and Victoria herself gave and wore hair jewelry throughout her life. From the moment of her betrothal to Albert she was never without a lock of his hair on her person. An entry in her journal reports that Empress Eugénie of France (married to Napoleon III) was "touched to tears when I gave her a bracelet with my hair."

By the mid-nineteenth century hair was no longer used merely to form pleasing designs or pictures under glass; it was used to make entire pieces of jewelry. It was boiled, weighted, glued, and strengthened with horsehair; it was braided, spun, woven, plaited, knitted, and crocheted; it was tipped, dotted, tasseled, caged, and secured with gold findings. It was shaped into hearts, anchors, and bows; it was coiled into serpents with cabochon garnet or ruby eyes; it was ballooned into wonderful netlike hollow openwork. Earrings were a lightweight dream to wear: long and dramatic, sometimes chandelier-shaped. Bracelets were fashioned like flexible woven ribbons with gold clasps or circlets of giant braided openwork. Watch chains were tightly coiled and sported dangling charms made of hair in the shape of hearts, anchors, crosses, and lyres. Women even made hair ornaments out of their own hair to enhance their elaborate Victorian coiffures. Often, more than one person's hair would be used in the making of a piece of jewelry, and some pieces utilized the hair of every member of the family!

Reverse side of a gold and enamel brooch, c. 1850, displaying a "family tree" made of hair.

This brings us to the one very pressing "hair" problem of the day; Unscrupulous hair workers were known to discard the hair of the loved one in favor of pretreated hair that was already in their possession. To discourage this devious practice, Victorian women were encouraged to make their own hair jewelry following the directions and patterns in the popular hair-working manuals of the day such as Alexanna Speight's *The Lock of Hair*. Unfortunately, this craft was no easy task to master,

Mid-Victorian openwork hair necklaces embellished with gold.

which probably explains all the poorly made hair jewelry that has survived to this day.

Hair jewelry was popular in France and the United States as well as England. An advertisement for a hair-working firm effervesces about its products in terms that would make a Madison Avenue copywriter feel right at home: "Hair is at once the most delicate and lasting of our materials and survives us, like love. It is so light, so gentle, so escaping from the idea of death, that, with a lock of hair belonging to a child or friend, we may almost look up to heaven . . . and say 'I have a piece of thee here, not unworthy of thy being now.'"

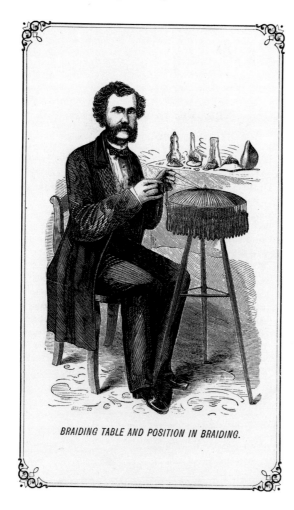

BRAIDING TABLE AND POSITION IN BRAIDING.

Victorian gentleman at a "braiding table," 1875.

Examples of hair jewelry in various colors. The bracelet in the center contains the hair of different family members.

Collecting and Care

hould you desire to buy some Victorian secondary jewelry, it might be advisable to remember the old adage: *More than one of anything is a collection*. But should you disregard this word of caution, here are some bits of information that might come in handy.

There are many reproductions on the market, so go slow, learn about your specialty, and do not be afraid to ask questions of dealers. This is their livelihood, and they should make it their business to know what they are selling. Never buy anything without a receipt that describes what the item is, what it is made of, and when it was made. If you find that the dealer's receipt is incorrect and that you no longer want to own the piece as a result of this, do not hesitate to bring it back

An array of Scottish agate figural jewelry.

and ask for a refund or credit. Any dealer worth his salt will want to accommodate you. This policy, however, may not extend to the condition of the piece. It is up to you, the customer, to inspect the article thoroughly. Obviously, if you are buying a piece as an investment, it should be perfect and unrepaired. But if you're buying it to wear, or just because you love it, you may decide to buy it "as is." Many dealers do not want to be bothered repairing every little evidence of wear and have priced their less-than-perfect pieces accordingly. One rule of thumb is that if you feel you are getting a real bargain, be sure to look the piece over thoroughly. It may not be as much of a bargain as you think.

Although most Victorian secondary jewelry is not signed, some of the silver or silver-and-agate pieces are hallmarked, and these assayer marks have acted as a protection for consumers for centuries. Hallmarks show that a piece of jewelry has been tested at an official assay office and certify an article's content and purity. Great Britain's hallmarks include a maker's mark, an assay office mark, and a silver standard mark. You can obtain a book identifying British and French hallmarks at any bookstore with a good antiques section. More rarely, one can find the diamond-shaped British Registry mark (known colloquially as a kite mark) on British goods manufactured and patented between 1842 and 1883. The Registry mark, which can tell you the exact day, month, and year a piece was registered, is in code but it can be deciphered. Michael Poynder's *Price Guide to Jewellery* can help you to interpret the code. That a piece has a Registry mark or a hallmark does not make it in and of itself better than another piece (quality, design, and workmanship being the variables) but they are good things to find on good pieces of jewelry.

You can find Victorian jewelry almost anywhere: in expensive department stores, in antique shops, at antique shows in the country as well as in the city, at local tag sales, flea markets, and secondhand stores. Naturally, the quality and rarity of pieces vary accordingly. But it *is*

A wearable collection of niello chatelaines.

Turn-of-the-century niello and pink gold "star" jewelry with an Edwardian look.

possible to find an amazing gem for very little money, if one is sharp of eye and persistent. For a true collector, the fabulous find is the ultimate serendipity.

CARE OF YOUR JEWELRY

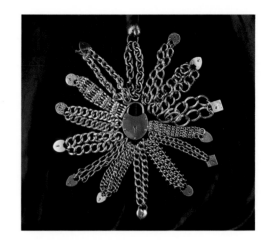

A roundup of padlock bracelets.

Silver

Silver is easy to care for and usually requires nothing more than a touch-up from time to time with a good silver-polishing cloth. If a piece is really tarnished, you can give it a soaking in soapy water with a little ammonia added. Avoid dipping cleaners—they can remove almost all the age and character from a piece. Silver polishes can also be a problem; if the piece has a great deal of detail, the polish tends to get stuck in the crevices and can be extremely difficult to remove. A silver-polishing cloth works best because it leaves a little oxidation on a piece exactly where it should be, in those hard-to-get-at places. It makes a piece shine but also lets it "show its age."

Never use anything but a silver-polishing cloth on niello. It has a baked-on enamel finish that can be worn away by polishes.

Stone

The care of agate can be trickier than that of silver because the shellac that was used to glue the stones in place over a hundred years ago tends to dry out over time, causing stones to come loose and drop out. Should you decide to collect agate jewelry, you may want to line up a local jeweler who has access to a stonecutter and stones. Otherwise there is little to do but run a polishing cloth over the silver setting from time to time.

A grouping of Victorian anchor brooches
in a variety of secondary materials surrounding
a nineteenth-century anchor pincushion
made of shells.

Steel

Cut steel, Berlin iron, and gunmetal can all fall prey to rust if they are exposed to damp or wet conditions. Once rusted, a piece is very hard, if not impossible, to clean. A toothbrush, not too hard, can sometimes remove surface rust from cut steel. Some books suggest brushing cut steel with ordinary chromium cleanser, leaving it to dry, then brushing it with a clean brush and polishing it with a soft cloth, but in our experience this has not often helped. Sometimes a dedicated scraping with one's fingernail works better. It has been said that jewelry repair people have a "trade secret" method of cleaning and polishing cut steel, so perhaps it is best to leave it to an expert. If you have a rusty piece of Berlin iron or gunmetal, try a light wiping with kerosene or oil.

Sentiment

Tortoiseshell, piqué, gutta-percha, and bog oak all enjoy a good mineral oil bath or wiping from time to time since these materials tend to dry out and look parched. Do not leave gutta-percha out in the sun: It turns from black to brown. If you have already done this, mineral oil may be able to revive and darken it. To restore the shine to jet, wash it gently with soap and water. If that does not do it, a microcrystalline wax cleaner/polish such as Renaissance can give jet a lovely sheen. We have been told that jet responds to a professional buffing from a good jewelry repair person. Hair jewelry may be cleaned by using a soft eyelash brush and a little soap and water, but go gently and make sure to dry it thoroughly. Never buy hair jewelry that is in bad condition. If your hair jewelry has a little "frizzing," try a small amount of hairspray to secure it.

Out in the antiques marketplace, try to become familiar with the type of jewelry you want to collect. Study it carefully, notice the findings, pin

Detail of two agate snake bracelets.

backs, clasps, and peculiarities that are the signposts of authenticity. Learn to recognize quality and to avoid pieces that are suspiciously new-looking, that have no signs of wear. Look for signed, hallmarked, and registered pieces. In bracelets, look for pairs; like complete suites of jewelry, they are always more valuable than singles. Finally, buy the things that really appeal to you and become you, and do not buy something just because someone else values it. In this way, your collection will be an extension of your own unique personality and afford you years and years of enjoyment.

Happy hunting and good luck!

Bibliography

BOOKS

Agates. London: Natural Museum Publications, 1989.

Armstrong, Nancy. *Victorian Jewelry*. London: Cassell and Collier Macmillan, 1976.

Bain, Robert. *The Clans and Tartans of Scotland*. London and Glasgow: Collins, 1938.

Becker, Vivienne. *Antique and Twentieth Century Jewellery*. Colchester, England: N.A.G. Press, 1987.

————. *Fabulous Fakes*. London: Grafton Books, 1988.

Black, J. Anderson. *A History of Jewelry*. New York: Park Lane, 1974.

Bradford, Ernle. *English Victorian Jewellery*. London: Spring Books, 1967.

Burgess, Fred. *Antique Jewelry and Trinkets*. New York: Tudor Publishing.

Bury, Shirley. *Sentimental Jewellery*. London: Her Majesty's Stationery Office, 1984.

Campbell, Mark. *Self-Instructor on the Art of Hair Work*. New York and Chicago: M. Campbell, 1867.

Chambers, Robert. *Traditions of Edinburgh*. London: W. & R. Chambers.

Clifford, Anne. *Cut-Steel and Berlin Iron Jewellery*. Bath, England: Adams and Dart, 1971.

Cooper, Diana, and Norman Battershill. *Victorian Sentimental Jewellery*. Plymouth, England: Latimer Trend and Co., Ltd, 1972.

Curran, Mona. *Collecting Antique Jewellery*. New York: Emerson Books, 1963.

Dent, Hubert. *Piqué: A Beautiful Minor Art*. London: Connoisseur Books, 1923.

Egger, Gerhart. *Generations of Jewelry*. Philadelphia: Schiffer, 1984.

Evans, Joan. *A History of Jewellery, 1100–1870*. New York: Dover Publications, 1970.

Flower, Margaret. *Victorian Jewelry*. London: Cassell and Co., 1951.

Gere, Charlotte. *Victorian Jewellery Design*. London: Kimber and Co., 1972.

Gere, Charlotte, and Geoffrey C. Munn. *Artists' Jewellery of the Pre-Raphaelite and Arts and Crafts Movements*. Woodbridge, England: Antique Collectors' Club, 1989.

Goldemberg, Rose Leiman. *Antique Jewelry: A Practical and Passionate Guide*. New York: Crown Publishers, 1976.

James, Duncan. *Old Jewellery*. Aylesbury, England: Shire Publications, 1989.

Kendall, Hugh. *The Story of Whitby Jet*. Whitby, England: Whitby Museum.

MacKay, James. *Rural Crafts in Scotland*. London: Robert Hale and Co., 1976.

Marquardt, Brigitte. *Schmuck*. Munich, Germany: Kunst & Antiquitäten, 1983.

Muller, Helen. *Jet Jewellery and Ornaments*. Aylesbury: Shire Publications, 1980.

Newman, Harold. *An Illustrated Dictionary of Jewelry*. New York: Thames and Hudson, 1981.

O'Day, Deirdre. *Victorian Jewellery*. London: Charles Letts Books, 1974.

Percival, MacIver. *Chats on Old Jewellery and Trinkets*. London: T. Fisher Unwin, 1912.

Peter, Mary. *Collecting Victorian Jewellery*. London: MacGibbon & Kee, 1970.

Pound, Reginald. *Queen Victoria*. London: Heron Books, 1970.

Poynder, Michael. *The Price Guide to Jewellery*. Woodbridge, England: Antique Collectors' Club, 1976.

Scarisbrick, Diana. *Jewellery*. London: Batsford, 1984.

Smith, Janet Adam. *Life among the Scots*. London: Collins, 1946.

Speight, Alexanna. *The Lock of Hair*. London, 1871.

Tait, Hugh, ed. *The Art of the Jeweller: A Catalogue of the Hull-Grundy Gift to the British Museum*. London: British Museum Publications, 1984.

CATALOGS

The Crystal Palace Exhibition, Illustrated Catalogue, London 1851. Reprint of the *Art Journal* special issue. New York: Dover Publications, 1970.

Great Exhibition of the Works of the Industry of All Nations, 1851. London, 1851.

The Jeweler's Eye. Yonkers, N.Y.: Hudson River Museum, 1986.

William Ernst Moutoux' Illustrated Catalogue of Hair Jewellery. New York: R. A. Welcke, 1883.

PERIODICALS

Victorian publications:

Godey's Lady's Book, Godey's Magazine, Harper's Bazaar, Illustrated London News, Queen, Jeweller's Weekly, Parisienne Illustrated Review, Young Ladies' Journal, Illustrated Household Magazine, Illustrated Exhibitor, Bon Accord (a Scottish journal).

Modern magazines:

Antique Collector, Antiques and Collecting, Spinning Wheel, Antique Collecting, Heritage.

Sources

Brian & Lynn Holmes, Grays Antique Market, London: pp. 24–25 (various pieces), 43, 72 (left), 73 (various pieces), 77 (bottom), 82 (brooch on top), 88, 89 (top right and bottom right), 92 (top: bracelet)

Butler & Wilson, London and Los Angeles: pp. 11 (bracelets, middle and right), 35 (top), 60, 64 (bottom: all but brooch on left), 67 (bottom), 69 (right), 70 (top), 94 (bottom: brooch), 95

Julie Seitzman Antique Jewelry, New York City: pp. 6, 13, 19, 26, 28 (left), 29 (top), 34 (bracelet), 46, 68, 69 (left), 93 (left: butterfly and arrow brooches), 96–97 (various pieces)

Justine S. Mehlman, Washington, D.C.: pp. 78 (brooch), 89 (top left), 93 (right), 105 (bracelet), 106 (brooch), 137 (bird and butterfly brooches)

James II Galleries Ltd, New York City: pp. 64 (top), 86, 96–97 (various pieces), 106 (earrings), 129 (right: bog oak bracelet), 146 (bow bracelet)

Angela Kramer: pp. 32 (amethyst brooch), 34 (cape pins), 92, 108 (ring), 134 (2nd, 3rd, and 4th bracelets from left), 137 (earrings)

Jacqueline Jacoby, Chelsea Galleries, Portobello Road, London: pp. 30 (left), 62, 67 (top: two brooches on left), 130, 138 (earrings)

Edith Weber & Co., Place des Antiquaires, New York City: pp. 112, 113 (top), 140

Kentshire Galleries, New York City: pp. 12 (brooch), 44 (bottom), 131 (bottom), 137 (oval brooch)

Kentshire at Bergdorf Goodman, New York City: pp. 44 (top), 78 (vertical bracelet), 91 (earrings)

Pam & Doug Brown, Westbourne Grove Arcade, Portobello Road, London: pp. 11 (bracelet on left), 66 (top and bottom)

Madeleine C. Popper, Grays Mews Antique Market, London: pp. 2 (various pieces), 96–97 (various pieces), 104 (top), 114 (left)

Eureka Antiques, Geoffrey Van Arcade, Portobello Road, London: pp. 12 (bracelet), 58 (left), 64 (bottom: brooch on left), 67 (top: brooch on right)

Jo & Olly, R.B.R. Group, Grays Antique Market, London: pp. 81 (top), 82 (brooch on bottom), 94 (top: brooch), 110

Joan Maxwell, London: pp. 33, 77 (top), 89 (bottom left)

Linda Morgan, The Mall, Camden Passage, London: pp. 128 (left and right), 138 (necklace)

Abacus Antiques, Grays Antique Market, London: pp. 24–25 (various pieces), 73 (various pieces)

Conyngham-Hynes, Grays Antique Market, London: pp. 2 (various pieces), 96–97 (various pieces)

Allison Massey, Grays Mews Antique Market, London: p. 20 (left)

Renee Lewis: p. 32 (everything but amethyst brooch)

Betty Brooks: p. 75 (bottom: brooch)

Patricia Funt Gallery, New York City: p. 91 (bracelet)

Barbara Brooks Jackson, Silver Spring, Maryland: p. 93 (left: circle pin)

Six Sept, New York City: p. 101 (left)

Amy Brown, New York City: p. 101 (right: heel ornaments)

Benita Berman: p. 105 (brooch and necklace)

Uniquities, South Orange, N.J.: pp. 104 (bottom), 122, 127 (right)

Olivia Collings, Bond Street Antique Centre, London: p. 111

The Spare Room Antiques, Baltimore, Maryland: p. 113 (bottom: bracelet)

Hancocks & Co., London: pp. 115 (hat pins), 116 (brooch)

Terry Rodgers, Manhattan Art and Antiques Center, New York City: p. 126

The Antique Jewel Box™, Burke, Virginia: p. 131 (top)

Eleanor Davidov: p. 139 (top)

Eugenie Benser, Baltimore, Maryland: p. 132

Antonia and Gary Blucher: p. 10 (left)

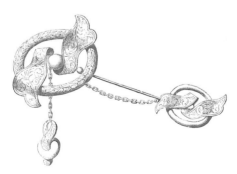

Index